South Dublin –

How to get by on, like, €10,000 a day

Edited by Ross O'Carroll-Kelly   *0 171810*

Contributors
JP Conroy,
Fionn de Barra,
Christian Forde and
Oisinn Wallace

PENGUIN
BOOKS

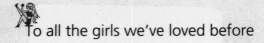

To all the girls we've loved before

PENGUIN BOOKS

Published by the Penguin Group
Penguin Books Ltd, 80 Strand, London WC2R 0RL, England
Penguin Group (USA), Inc., 375 Hudson Street, New York, New York 10014, USA
Penguin Group (Canada), 90 Eglinton Avenue East, Suite 700, Toronto, Ontario,
Canada M4P 2Y3 (a division of Pearson Penguin Canada Inc.)
Penguin Ireland, 25 St Stephen's Green, Dublin 2, Ireland (a division of Penguin Books Ltd)
Penguin Group (Australia), 250 Camberwell Road, Camberwell, Victoria 3124, Australia
(a division of Pearson Australia Group Pty Ltd)
Penguin Books India Pvt Ltd, 11 Community Centre,
Panchsheel Park, New Delhi – 110 017, India
Penguin Group (NZ), 67 Apollo Drive, Rosedale, North Shore 0632, New Zealand
(a division of Pearson New Zealand Ltd)
Penguin Books (South Africa) (Pty) Ltd, 24 Sturdee Avenue, Rosebank,
Johannesburg 2196, South Africa

Penguin Books Ltd, Registered Offices: 80 Strand, London WC2R 0RL, England

www.penguin.com

First published as *Ross O'Carroll Kelly's Guide to South Dublin* by Penguin Ireland 2007
This edition published as *South Dublin* in Penguin Books 2008
1

Penguin Ireland thanks O'Brien Press for its agreement to Penguin Ireland using
the same design approach and typography, and the same artist, as O'Brien Press
used in the first four Ross O'Carroll-Kelly titles

Set in Monotype Frutiger
Typeset by Rowland Phototypesetting Ltd, Bury St Edmunds, Suffolk
Printed in England by Clays Ltd, St Ives plc

ISBN: 978–1–844–88164–2

www.greenpenguin.co.uk

Penguin Books is committed to a sustainable future
for our business, our readers and our planet.
The book in your hands is made from paper
certified by the Forest Stewardship Council.

Contents

The Authors 🌴

Ross O'Carroll-Kelly An outstanding rugby talent, Ross captained Castlerock College to victory in the Leinster Schools Senior Cup in 1999. George Hook described him as 'the player most likely to make the breakthrough next year' every Christmas between 2000 and 2005, and it has often been said that he could have been where Brian O'Driscoll is today had he not been such a Jack the Lad. Not that he's complaining. He's enjoyed his life, and not even his marriage in 2003 to Sorcha Lalor – the on-off love of his life – has affected his prolific strike-rate with the ladies. He still does more than alroysh, thank you very much. He is the father of two children, one of each – that is to say, one skobie kid and one normal one. Honor (2) is his daughter by Sorcha and Ronan (9) is his son by Tina, a total Natalie he boned at the age of sixteen while on a cultural exchange programme with a school on the Northside. He has been barred from more than half of the pubs and clubs mentioned in this book. He received a six-figure advance to write this guide to South Dublin and spent it while his friends did all the research for €5,000 each. He lives in Blackrock. The only relevant detail in his biography, though, is that his old man is worth €57 million.

JP Conroy After completing school, JP went into property, joining his father's estate agency, Hook, Lyon & Sinker, in Ballsbridge. He very quickly established a reputation for sharp practices, which earned warnings about his future conduct from the IAVI, the Advertising Standards Authority and the Gardaí in Donnybrook. It was JP who first called Tullamore 'the Gateway to Dublin' and described a house in Monaghan as being 'just an hour from the capital'. It was – the capital of Northern Ireland. In 2004 he found God and turned his back on his old life. He is currently studying for the priesthood.

Fionn de Barra After gaining maximum points in his Leaving Certificate, Fionn studied English and Psychology at UCD. In 2003 and 2004 he spent six months in France, studying the life and work of the French poet Arthur Rimbaud for a Ph.D. He is currently doing a Masters in Anthropological Studies at Trinity College, Dublin. By the time he's done, he's expected to be too qualified to work at anything. His hobbies are poetry, history and languages. He has not had his Nat King Cole for years.

Christian Forde His bebo site describes him as the biggest *Star Wars* fan in the world – and restraining orders from eight former cast members attest to that. A harmless sociopath,

Christian married Lauren Coghlan-O'Hara, a surprisingly normal girl, in 2006. They have a house in Dublin 4, though Christian continues to live in a galaxy far, far away.

 Oisinn Wallace After a year in Sports Management – the only course in UCD that would take him after he failed his Leaving Cert. – Oisinn gave it all up to pursue the career he really wanted: developing ladies' perfumes. Working night and day in a makeshift laboratory at the back of his parents' house, he created a unique smell, for which Hugo Boss paid him a record €1 million advance in 2004. *Eau d'Affluence* was launched in Milan a year later. Never one to rest on his laurels, Oisinn soon hit on a new business idea – scented holy water. *Love One Another As I Have Loved Yuzu* and *Take Up Thy Bergamot and Walk* are set to hit supermarket shelves soon. Oisinn is big right now – he's 17 stone – and half the international modelling world is trying to get into his 38-inch chinos. It's a pity he prefers ditchpigs.

How to Use This Guide ⃞Ⴑ

This travel guide is divided into three main content areas. The first section is called 'The Basics'. It contains all the information you'll need to gain an understanding of this extraordinary region and its people, thus enabling you to get the most from your visit. The second section takes you on a journey through each of South Dublin's eight districts, offering in-depth accounts of the sights, practical tips on activities and up-to-the-minute reviews of the most expensive places to stay, eat and drink. Each of the book's authors offers his tuppence-worth on his own particular areas of expertise in the regular 'A Word From' pieces. The final section is the 'ThesauRoss', a dictionary of words and terms commonly used in South Dublin. It will give you a better understanding of what the fock everyone is banging on about.

Introduction 🐦

Nestled between the grim boglands of Wicklow and the filthy squalor of North and West Dublin is a land of **untold beauty and wealth**, which boasts more millionaires per square acre than Manhattan, where the pace of life is positively Californian, where males address one another by their surnames, where a sense of community is non-existent – and where the sun never stops shining . . .

In spite of all this, South Dublin – or 'the saithsade' in the local parlance – remains one of the world's most overlooked holiday destinations. Yet visitors to this tranquil, sun-kissed paradise find a land full of surprises – not all of them involving their **credit card statements**.

South Dublin is so much more than home to the **world's most expensive cappuccino**. Visitors are often surprised to discover that the Southside has a cultural history dating back more than **twenty years**. This is reflected not only in its glorious art, music and theatre, but in the Mock-Tudor, Mock-Gothic and Mock-Georgian architecture with which it has become synonymous.

For the gastronome, too, South Dublin has much to recommend it. Where else would you find a restaurant that effects the dining mannerisms of the eighteenth-century French aristocracy, or a restaurant where steak, chips and onion rings for two will set you back a couple of hundred euro? Then there are the **gourmet food shops**, selling everything from Imperial Beluga Black Sea caviar to low-carb, sugar-free truffles. Terrine of duck *foie gras*, gluten-free shortbread and elk summer sausage are as plentiful on the Southside as **crack cocaine** is on the Northside.

Bathed by the warm currents of the Gulf Stream and the North Atlantic Drift, South Dublin has a **hot, humid climate**, not unlike that of the Cayman Islands, with whom Southsiders share a natural affinity. Add in the 365 days of **guaranteed sunshine** per year and it's not difficult to see why houses here are changing hands for the equivalent of the GNP of a small, backward country, such as Albania, Chad . . . or the rest of Ireland.

South Dublin is still technically part of the Irish Republic, although to all intents and purposes it is a **sovereign state unto itself**, with its own language, rituals and customs. Prosperity has accelerated the progress towards full **secession**, which, it is predicted, could take place before the year 2020.

South Dublin is not only the cradle of the Celtic Tiger, it is also a land rich in cultural diversity, where barristers live next door to stockbrokers, where judges live next door to businessmen and where heart surgeons live side by side with brain surgeons. Furthermore, its cultural horizons are forever expanding. Take a minute to sit in Hilper's or Starbucks and – providing you can overcome the language barrier – listen to the young **intellectuals** from UCD and DBS debate the big issues of the day: who will win *Big Brother VIII*, how many points are in a skinny peach and raspberry muffin and what is the best way to apply Piz Buin to one's feet without getting streaks?

Zero-tolerance policing and strict border controls have brought about the almost total eradication of crime, apart from **petty offences** such as tax evasion, planning corruption, money laundering and other misdemeanours.

South Dubliners love their **sport** – mostly the ones they're good at. The area, for instance, boasts more **yachts** per head of population than Monte Carlo.

An estimated 40 per cent of South Dublin is made up of **golf courses**. That figure is set to increase to as much as 60 per cent as rising prices force what remains of the area's **indigenous working-class population** out into the townships of North and West Dublin, or further south to Wicklow and Wexico, leaving vast swathes of land to be developed to answer the pressing demand for more **room in which to golf**. The national obsession, however, is rugby, and excitement reaches

fever-pitch whenever the famous Leinster team plays, with fans driven to such delirious excesses as **actually going to the games** and occasionally **cheering**.

Visitors to South Dublin should take time to sample its wonderfully vibrant nightlife. The Southside is home to two of the world's most exclusive nightclubs. No famous visitor to Ireland is permitted to leave without spending an evening in either **Lillie's Bordello** or **Renards**. For sybarites, there are literally dozens of fashionable fleshpots where the Celtic Tiger's young cubs gather to pout and strut their stuff like catwalk models. The city caters for revellers of all ages, from the celebrated **Wesley Disco**, where to have knickers on is to be overdressed, to the *über*-cool **Ice Bar** and its famous range of outrageously priced Mojitos. And don't be dissuaded by a refusal from the door staff of a pub or club. This is simply an elaborate ritual that 'bouncers' – or admission consultants, as they prefer to be known – engage in to find out whether you're **pissed** or, worse, **working class, like them**. After indulging them for a few minutes, you'll eventually be let in, providing, of course, that you're neither.

For the overseas visitor there is no end of things to do. You can spend an afternoon in **Bel-Éire**, gazing at the gated mansions where Bono, Van Morrison and Eddie Irvine occasionally live. Enjoy an afternoon's **sailing** through the tranquil, pollution-free waters off Sandycove. Or why not while away an afternoon over a tall, skinny, no-whip **vanilla latte** in any of the wonderfully soulless chain coffee shops that have sprung up all over the Southside in recent years?

Few places on Earth can match the raw and intense beauty of this region, which has managed to strike the perfect **environmental balance** between that which has been sculpted by nature and that which has been fashioned by man. Whether you're riding the surf down on Monkstown beach, or riding a heavily Botoxed girl with a fashionably obscure Irish name after half-a-dozen Mint Juleps in Lillie's, you'll be bowled over by its unique sense of aesthetic equilibrium.

South Dublin has something for **travellers** of all kinds, except the ones with a capital T, who are advised to park their caravans somewhere more appropriate, such as Tallaght or Finglas.

As the furnace that fired Ireland's miracle economic turnaround, South Dublin is *the* place to do **business** in Europe, and hundreds of thousands of business types flock here every year, hoping some of the entrepreneurial energies of financial titans like **Sean Dunne** and **Denis O'Brien** will rub off on them. Thanks to men like these, as well as their *über*-rich friends, the area bristles with economic good health. Recent constructions, such as the **Dundrum Town Centre**, and the annexation of the South Inner City area by the computer industry – **Googleland** – have given this already modern, cosmopolitan corner of the world a new, twenty-first-century dimension. It's predicted that **Ballsbridge** will soon become a city in itself – South Dublin's very own gleaming capital, with shiny new corporate skyscrapers bearing down on dowdy old Dublin City.

Southsiders take justifiable pride in their environment. They **recycle** more than any other people in Europe, and what waste can't be reused is left outside their homes in wheelie bins, taken away and dumped on the Northside, or in a large municipal dump in north Wicklow known as **Bray**. Whales, dolphins and seals frolic in the cleanest waters in Europe, off the Southside coast. South Dublin's only indulgence with regard to pollutants is the ubiquitous **SUV**, which has become as recognizable a symbol of the area as the yellow taxi is of New York.

For all their self-confidence, South Dubliners can often seem quite reserved. Don't worry, it's only **rudeness** and just takes a little getting used to. They'll generally show little or no interest in you until they establish some common connection; then they'll be as false and insincere to you as they are to each other.

All this – and shopping! South Dublin is a consumer's paradise, with thousands of shops just waiting to take your money – and look sulky about it in the process.

It's little wonder that stars such as Bono and Brian O'Driscoll have chosen South Dublin as their home over the South of France.

There's never been a better time to visit the Southside. This sun-drenched, fun-loving, bountiful playground is just waiting for you to arrive . . . with your plastic.

The Basics ○

South Dublin is a beautiful, sun-kissed oasis in the North Atlantic, situated just 67 miles (105 km) off the coast of Britain. It is 1,224 miles (1,931 km) from **Tuscany**, 4,312 miles (6,920 km) from **Barbados** and 6,107 miles (9,656 km) from the **Maldives** . . .

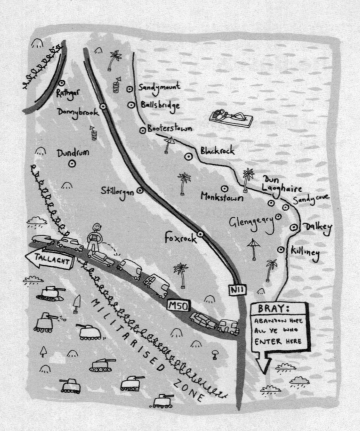

Geography

South Dublin is, at the time of writing, still attached to the Ireland landmass. It is located between North Dublin and the counties of Wicklow and Kildare, and affords spectacular sea views, as well as access to every modern facility. Defined to the north by the River Liffey and to the east by the Irish Sea, its exact area is uncertain, as its southern and western boundaries are open to interpretation. A number of **estate agents** have suggested it stretches as far south as **Bray** and as far west as **Tallaght**, but have subsequently been prosecuted under the **Trades Description Act**. For the vast majority of Southsiders, anything south of Killiney and west of Dundrum is not South Dublin but **either 'Bogland' or 'the Northside'**.

The borders have been further confused by the growing prosperity of a number of coastal suburbs north of the Liffey, including Howth, Sutton, Portmarnock and Clontarf, which regard themselves as being more 'Southside' than areas such as **Ballybrack and Sallynoggin**, which are technically within the boundaries of South Dublin.

Recent years have seen the notional line that divides the city socially turn 90° on its axis, so that the conflict is now between east and west rather than south and north. Many, however, regard being a Southsider as not so much a geographical question as a **state of mind**.

South Dublin's unique position on the map means it enjoys hot and humid summers and warm weather for the remainder of the year. While the rest of Ireland suffers through icy winters and more than 300 days of rainfall a year, the North Atlantic Drift ensures that the

A WORD FROM FIONN

Postcodes are very important to South Dubliners because they determine which social caste you belong to – Dublin 4 and Dublin 18 being the most prestigious. The postcode system is relatively simple: Southside numbers are even; Northside numbers are odd. It was originally designed to allow employers to weed out job applicants from the Northside before they reached interview stage. There's only one exception to the odd/even rule and that's Áras an Uachtaráin, the residence of the President of Ireland. It's on the wrong side of the river, but is classified as Dublin 8. So Mrs Mary McAleese is the only Northsider who's allowed to call herself a Southsider. And you wouldn't blame her either.

temperature in South Dublin rarely drops below 30°C, **even in December**. It represents one of the world's most significant temperature anomalies relative to latitude and goes some way towards explaining the proliferation of **palm trees** in South Dublin, as well as other plants more commonly associated with tropical climes.

History

The earliest recorded reference to South Dublin, as distinct from the rest of the county, is in the writings of **Claudius Ptolemaeus**, the astronomer and cartographer. Around the year AD 140, he referred to it as *Eblana Nosupitas*, literally **'Land of People With Their Noses in the Air'**.

The settlement of Dublin is thought to date back to the first century BC. The name is an Anglicized version of Dubh Linn, which is Gaelic for **Blackpool**, and the continued use of the name today reflects the poorer side of the city's love affair with **slot-machines,**

deep-fried food and walking around on sunny days with their tops off.

Even in those pre-Christian times the division lines between North and South were being drawn. The more prosperous people settled south of the Liffey and considered the population on the other side of the river – who were proud, rather than ashamed, of being descended from the invading Celts – to be **uncouth**, with **inferior intelligence** and low standards of **personal hygiene**. Northsiders were distinguished then, as today, by their **wispy moustaches** and **pigeon-like gait**, and they remain true to their Celtic ancestry to this day, with most of them supporting a Scottish **soccer** team that bears the name.

Most Southsiders were keen to put as much distance between themselves and their Celtic past as they could, especially when they started to make serious amounts of wonga, which was the currency in Ireland's earliest **monied economy**. While Northsiders eked out a meagre living from hunting, fishing and farming, Southsiders became **traders**, **brehons** or, as they're known today, **senior counsels**.

Fifth-century Ireland was divided into a number of kingdoms and the earliest record of South Dublin being defined as distinct from North Dublin dates from this time. **St Patrick's** efforts to introduce Christianity to South Dublin at this time were frustrated when, according to legend, he was told by the king, 'We're

loaded – what the fock do we need to be praying for?',
at which point Patrick switched his efforts to the poorer
and more malleable population on the other side of the
river. Christianity still thrives in North Dublin to this day,
while South Dublin continues to worship **wonga**.

Ireland's tradition of **storytelling** first took root
during this period. In the centuries before the arrival of
the high-definition plasma widescreen television, there
was little to do at night but sit around recounting
stories of great events, vainglorious battles and tribal
histories, most of which were **total bullshit**. Yet
South Dubliners had their folk heroes, like everyone
else. The most famous, recorded by scholars on a
vellum manuscript that survives to this day, involved
a giant named Oisún, who, despite **horrific facial
deformities**, excelled at a type of kick-and-rush
ballgame and is said to have bedded **1,000 women**.
The legend is considered to be the origin of the
Leinster Schools Senior Cup.

Ireland missed out on the civilizing influence of the
Romans, and by the eighth century the place had gone
to ruin, with **killings** and **tribal warfare** taking place
on a scale that would embarrass some of North Dublin's
most infamous suburbs today. South Dubliners were
often heard to say, 'What this place needs is a good
invasion.'

They got two – first the **Vikings**, then the **Normans**.
Despite sacking, raping and pillaging the country, at

least they made the streets safer to walk at night.

The Northside resisted the Viking invasion, and, in 1014, **Brian Boru**, who had set himself up as High King of Ireland, won a decisive victory over the Norsemen at **Clontarf**. Typically, South Dubliners weren't too concerned, once the trouble was kept to the other side of the city.

The Normans arrived in 1169, and within a year the warrior **Strongbow** had captured all of Dublin and married a girl called **Aoife**. His high approval rating in South Dublin is reflected in the continuing popularity of his wife's name in affluent Southside areas today.

Outside of South Dublin there was huge resistance to the Norman conquest, especially after the arrival of Henry II in 1171, which marked the beginning of eight centuries of Anglo-Irish conflict. South Dublin welcomed the invaders from across the water, however, and intermarriage resulted in the Norman conquerors becoming **more South Dublin than the South Dubliners themselves**. Happy to be subjugated, most of the natives began speaking with clipped, English accents and developed themselves into a **landlord class**.

For eight centuries the English were a largely benign presence in Ireland, apart from a few isolated incidents, such as the **Plantations**, the massacres by **Oliver Cromwell** and his Ironsides, and the **Penal Laws**, none of which received much publicity in South Dublin. The area was also unaffected by the **Potato Famine** of 1845–9, which saw one million Irish men and women die of starvation and a further million emigrate, mainly to America. South Dubliners experienced no such horrors, having long since switched to a **richer and more varied diet** that included wild salmon, roast pheasant, wild boar and various multi-coloured pastas.

The Famine was a watershed in Irish history, as the inadequacy of the British government's response left an enduring **legacy of bitterness** that fired the demand for independence. South Dublin did not agree with the notion of autonomy from Britain, an attitude that is still common to many Southsiders. The area resisted **Home Rule** more vigorously than Ulster's Protestants and played no part in the **War of Independence** (1919–21). The **Easter Rising** in 1916 was also a purely Northside affair. The guns were landed in Howth by the **Irish Volunteers**, who took over a number of key administrative buildings, most of them north of the Liffey. Heavy artillery was deployed against the rebel strongholds. Hundreds of shells were fired at the GPO on O'Connell Street, causing **millions of pounds worth of improvements**. South Dublin opposed the Treaty that followed the War of Independence, believing, like Éamon de Valera, that its future lay as part of a thirty-two-county Republic – **under British rule**.

Modern History

South Dublin went into a collective sulk after Independence, but soon knuckled down and got on with doing what it does best – making **potloads of cash**. The rest of Ireland, finally free of **'the Brits'**, spent the next eighty years obsessing about them and engaging in lively debates about who hated **'them across the water'** the most. Meanwhile, South Dubliners eschewed bitterness, embraced education and began the transition from a mostly landlord class to a **diverse professional one**.

In 1939 Germany's invasion of Poland precipitated a conflict that killed 55 million people, involved an effort to exterminate the entire Jewish race, saw two Japanese cities vapourized and, by the time it ended six years later, left the threat of nuclear annihilation hanging over the Earth like the Sword of Damocles. The world called this horror the **Second World War**; Ireland called it **The Emergency**, making it sound rather like a **chip-pan fire**.

During the war, Ireland remained neutral – but neutral more on Hitler's side of things, what with them **hating the Brits and that**. South Dublin, on the other hand, stood four-square behind the Allies. When **Winston Churchill** considered a strategic invasion of

Ireland to take control of the so-called Treaty ports, the people of Dún Laoghaire were panting like a gaggle of prostitutes waiting for a naval ship to dock. Alas, Churchill changed his mind.

For once South Dublin found itself on the same side as the Catholic Church in the row that brought about the collapse of the inter-party government in 1951. The Minister for Health, Dr Noël Browne, proposed a **'Mother and Child Scheme'** that would give free medical care to expectant mothers and to children up to the age of sixteen years. He drew the ire of the all-powerful Catholic hierarchy, which felt the proposal interfered with the rights of the family and the individual. South Dubliners opposed it because they resented their tax money being spent on people who could afford cigarettes but couldn't afford **private health insurance**. The term **'parasites'** entered the South Dublin lexicon for the first time.

Ireland joined the **European Economic Community** in 1973, and, after twenty-five years of membership, the rest of the country finally started to enjoy the kind of lifestyle that South Dubliners had been enjoying for generations. **Germany, France** and the **'bloody Brits'** paid for Ireland's roads. **America** opened up lots of factories, giving hundreds of thousands of barely literate boggers jobs in manufacturing, thus saving them from a lifetime on **a milking stool**.

Now that it has the M50, the Luas light-rail system

and the new Dublin Port Tunnel, as well as plans for a rail link to the airport, an underground transport system and a new national sports stadium, Ireland is expected to be **very nice when it's finished**. South Dublin already is. Even before the upturn in Ireland's economy the area was ridiculously well off. The Celtic Tiger has simply made it rich beyond its dreams. In 2001 South Dublin was declared a **UNESCO Region of Extreme Affluence**.

How to Get There

Despite its wealth and prosperity, South Dublin does not yet have an airport of its own. If you intend travelling to Ireland on a commercial flight, remember you will be **landing on the Northside**. Don't be alarmed by the burning buildings and car chases you might see below you as the plane descends towards Dublin Airport. The M50 motorway, which was completed in June 2005, was built as a means of transporting visitors from the airport to the Southside as quickly as possible, without their having to witness any of the Northside's desperate squalor. Alternatively, you can fly to Britain, privately charter a **helicopter** or **small jet**, then land on any of the thousands of helipads or private airstrips that are scattered all over South Dublin.

In addition, Stena Sealink operates a **high-speed**

THE FATHER OF MODERN SOUTHSIDERS: DAVID McWILLIAMS

He's not only Ireland's cleverest man but its poshest, too. And just to send us goys even further over the edge with jealousy, he's also one of the sexiest, according to a poll in some women's magazine or other, proving that knowing loads of stuff isn't necessarily a turn-off for women.

The strawberry-blonde brainiac has been described as 'Eddie Hobbs with looks'. But, hailing from staunchly middle-class Dalkey, McWilliams is unlikely to advise anybody to scrabble around

trying to save 50 cents on a tankful of petrol, or to cross the Liffey to get the cheaper tea-towels in Guineys. While misery-guts Hobbs has tried to make a generation feel guilty for its profligacy with his catchphrase 'You're being ripped off!', the man who defined the Celtic Tiger generation in his bestselling book *The Pope's Children* would likely respond, 'So what, Dude? We can afford to be!'

Hard as it is to believe, McWilliams played soccer as a boy, much to the concern of his family. But, despite his early identity crisis, he has been flying high ever since. He was educated at Blackrock College, Trinity College and the College of Europe in the Belgian city of Bruges. From 1990 to 1993 he worked as an economist with the Central Bank, doing all sorts of boring stuff, before heading up the European Economics Department for UBS. More corporate high-flying followed in Paris and New York, before he finally appeared on our television screens as the presenter of TV3's *Agenda*, proving once and for all that economists don't have to be tedious old farts. Tens of thousands of men watched his interviews and said, 'No man could be that clever,' while women said, 'I wouldn't throw him out of bed for talking about carefully staged pre-releases of preference stock and notional rights issues.'

McWilliams has interviewed Mikhail Gorbachev, Hillary Clinton and Henry Kissinger, presented a morning drive-time show on NewsTalk 106 and hosted *The Big Bite*, a topical afternoon discussion programme on RTÉ television. He's well-known as a really good goy. And he has a holiday home in Croatia – the posh part, naturally – which he's prepared to let people use for free.

P.S. Don't ask to borrow McWilliams's gaff in the first two weeks in August. I usually have it then. – Ross

ferry service between Holyhead and Dún Laoghaire, in the heart of Dublin's Southside. Be warned, however, that the service tends to attract a lot of riff-raff, some enjoying what's known in the local argot as a **'booze cruise'**, others on their way to and from **Premiership soccer matches**. Even 100 minutes can seem like a lifetime when you're stuck on a boat with a bunch of people wearing Manchester United shirts, drinking cans of Tennent's and singing songs by **Aslan**.

The People

Being born in South Dublin is like holding a winning ticket in the lottery of life. So it's not surprising that the locals have adopted something of an island mentality. Visitors should be warned that Southsiders can often seem **rude to strangers** – and also to people they know. Bad manners is only a small part of the picture, however. They are generally a **fun-loving** people, whether soaking up the sun aboard a 60-ft oyster yacht off the coast of Dalkey, or watching proudly as little Hannah rides her dream pony Chestnut to victory in the local gymkhana.

With their appreciation of French food, Italian shirts and Caribbean holidays, Southsiders can justifiably claim to have been Ireland's first **multiculturalists**, long before the media ever discovered the term. No one has embraced the invasion of non-nationals quite like them – especially as immigrant workers are cheaper than Irish ones and tend to steal less.

South Dubliners have earned a reputation for intolerance due to their long-standing objections to the building of halting sites in their area. This is undeserved, however. They are, in fact, a very charitable people and there's nothing like a natural disaster in some far-flung country to bring out the kinder side of their nature.

NATIONAL ANTHEM
(to the tune of Go West by the Village People)

We're rich – and we know we are,
We're rich – and we know we are,
We're rich – and we know we are,
We're rich – and we know we are.

(instrumental)

We're rich – and we know we are,
We're rich – and we know we are,
We're rich – and we know we are,
We're rich – and we know we are.

Per capita, South Dublin contributed more money to the Asian tsunami and Turkish earthquake relief funds from **roulade sales** and **fashion shows** than any other nation on Earth.

Generally speaking, South Dublin **women** don't work, but they do keep busy, many of them enjoying hobbies such as **tennis, golf and having lunch**. There's little they enjoy more than getting together with 'the girls' for a good natter over a spinach, pecan and blue cheese quiche in **Avoca Handweavers**, or anywhere that serves posh food. They also tend to be very involved in their children's lives and like to consider themselves to be **best friends** with their daughters. And, like their daughters, they sure love to shop!

The **men** are usually very driven, both by their work and by the sporting achievements of their children, through whom they live out their own dreams vicariously. They drive Kompressors, speak with **upper-class English accents** and 'take' *The Irish Times* every day. Their dream in life is to play a round of golf with **Dermot Desmond**, **JP McManus** and **John Magnier**. Although they leave school, school never really leaves them, and they maintain an almost Masonic loyalty to their *alma mater* until the day they die.

It is a fact that South Dublin's young men – or **goys** – have two main preoccupations: rugby and girls. Their devotion to one and their studied disregard of the other is considered an index of their malehood. They are heavily influenced by American **jock culture**, and their language and rituals – high-fiving and calling each other 'Dude' – are informed by the high-school scene in America. **Adolescence** lasts much longer in South Dublin than in other parts of the developed world, often into the **mid thirties**, the age at which most eventually leave home and stop bleeding their parents dry.

As they have their own recondite language and accent, it's virtually impossible to understand **South Dublin girls** if you are an outsider. Remember, American sitcoms and dramas, such as *Friends*, *The OC* and *Desperate Housewives,* form the collective unconscious of the female 14–30 generation, which explains why most speak with **American accents** so pronounced that even Californians struggle to make sense of what they are saying.

South Dublin females enjoy a far broader **range of interests** than males do, including losing weight, boys, texting, shopping, losing weight to get boys, wearing pink, texting boys, shopping for clothes that make them look like they've lost weight, reading *Hello!* and *Heat*, shopping for pink clothes, saying 'OH MY GOD' a lot, as well as texting each other to report how much weight they've lost, how much shopping they've done and what boys they're interested in. To say that South Dublin girls learn to text in the **womb** is only a slight exaggeration. In fact, most children's clothes from the age of two up are made with a special pocket to accommodate a mobile phone:

South Dublin boys and girls are generally **stupid**,

 YUMMY-MUMMIES

They're in Pia Bang and Pamela Scott, trying on clothes designed for women twenty years their junior. They're in Laura Ashley, looking for a pale pink taffeta lamp to match the curtains in the guest bedroom. They're in Avoca Handweavers, eating sun-dried tomato, olive and ricotta-stuffed baked potatoes, pretending to be Protestants.

They're Yummy-Mummies.

They're in their fifties, but could pass for forty. They're well preserved to the point that the secret must be embalming fluid. They have two or three children of college-going age, and yet they've kept their figures intact and their pretty faces unlined. They use just the right amount of make-up. They smell of rose petals and lavender. They have young names, like Claire and Sarah. They play tennis. They drive SUVs and wear sunglasses on their heads. They are always smiling and never hassled.

They are little rays of sunshine that illuminate all our lives.

hence the proliferation of grind schools in the area. They seldom find this an obstacle to getting **good jobs**, though, which explains why South Dublin has the highest standard of living **relative to literacy** in the entire world.

Heroes of South Dublin Life ...

Brian O'Driscoll

Drico. The Dricster. BOD. God. Call him what you will, Brian O'Driscoll is Ireland's first rugby superstar of the professional age and a role model for all South Dublin males. The irony is that, despite the designer clobber and the signature Disney Club voice, O'Driscoll isn't from the Southside at all. In 2005, after almost a year of surveillance, a tabloid newspaper exposed his darkest secret – Ireland's inspirational captain is from Clontarf, on the city's Northside. However, a fly-on-the-wall

documentary about Ireland's 2007 Six Nations campaign revealed O'Driscoll imploring his team-mates, 'Oh, sure, we've been good – but we could be great!' and his

Southside credentials were immediately clear and, like Bono, he has used his enormous wealth to build himself a home on the right side of the city. Apart from that, there's not a lot more to say. A hat-trick of tries in Paris at the tender age of twenty; one of the greatest tries of all time for the Lions at twenty-one; Captain of Ireland at twenty-two; three Triple Crowns; cool cars; fit birds; Ireland's Sexiest Man award. His life story reads like every South Dublin adolescent's wettest dreams come true.

Robbie Fox

Bon viveur, raconteur and confidant to the stars, Robbie Fox is also the owner and gatekeeper of Renard's, Ireland's most exclusive nightclub. Everyone in South Dublin knows his face. The question is: does he know yours?

Liz O'Donnell

Her name literally means, 'Angel sent by God to make sure Southsiders never give up on democracy'. O'Donnell was a TD for South Dublin between 1992 and 2007, when the electorate decided that her work in the Oireachtas was done and she should spend a lot more time on television, where we can see her. O'Donnell represented the Irish government at the multi-party talks at Stormont that led to the Good Friday Agreement – snore! She is better known as the

poster girl for South Dublin's yummy-mummy
movement and a Paul Costelloe-dressed rebuttal to the
argument that women can't be brainy and beautiful.
Since she lost her seat in 2007, Dáil Éireann has
returned to being the world's third ugliest parliament –
after Turkmenistan and Westerm Samoa.

George Hook
For most South Dublin males 'Hooky' is the old man
they never had. The ursine sixty-something is not only

Ireland's most outspoken pundit and broadcaster, he's the quintessential South Dublin dad. In other words, he lives in Foxrock, he's not afraid to have his voice heard in public, and he's a member of Milltown Golf Club.

Sharon Ní Bheoláin
The RTÉ newsreader is more than just eye candy with an IQ of, well, something ridiculously high. She edges out fellow Bulletin Babes Gráinne Seoige and Claire Byrne as every South Dublin schoolboy's fantasy Irish teacher.

Graham Knuttel
Sylvester Stallone saw Knuttel's work on a visit to Ireland a few years ago and ordered just about every painting he had in his workshop. Now South Dublin can't get enough of his work either.

Sean Dunne
The man they call 'Dunner' is the CEO of D4 Inc. Nobody has ridden the wave of Ireland's economic miracle better than the Carlow-born quantity surveyor, who has amassed a vast fortune from property development since the 1990s. Lately, he's been buying up half of Ballsbridge and is rumoured to have plans for his own Trump Tower on the Jurys Hotel site. He has a house on Shrewsbury Road, a stunning wife, access to Aristotle Onassis's yacht, and he's good to charity. You'd have to hate him if he wasn't so nice.

... and anti-heroes 🄻

Michael O'Leary

Since becoming the Chief Executive of Ryanair in 1994,
the former Clongowes boy has shaken up the airline
industry with his abrasive, what-the-fock-do-you-
expect-at-these-prices? approach to business. Offering
flights for as little as €2, he has made mainland Europe
accessible for poor people. Paris, Rome and Venice are
now full of boggers and skobies – and for that, South
Dubliners will never forgive him.

Michael McDowell

The former Tánaiste, leader of the Progressive Demo-
crats and TD for Dublin South East made an enemy of
the Southside's youth when, as Minister for Justice, he
introduced a number of measures to curb underage and
binge drinking – two of South Dublin's most cherished
traditions. The loss of his Dáil seat in the 2007 general
election was his fitting reward.

TK Maxx

This chain of department stores has made its reputation
by selling brand-name clothing at ridiculously affordable
prices. As a result, Southsiders have lost their exclusive
claim on labels such as Ralph Lauren and Tommy

Hilfiger. Now every Anto in town can afford a designer shirt. It's little wonder that South Dubliners are using the term 'TK Maxx' as rhyming slang for a toilet, or **jacks**:

Flora and Fauna

South Dublin people love their animals, and there's no animal that receives more love than the **yappy dog**. The term is used to cover a number of breeds, but typically refers to any cantankerous, miniature-sized dog with silky hair that barks incessantly and at an annoyingly high pitch. These include **Pomeranians** and **toy poodles**. They are often named Saskia or Poppet, fed like family members and indulged like children. They are commonly seen being carried by rich, middle-aged women, appearing to grow out of the armpits of their fur coats. Their natural belligerence and tendency to snap at **anyone who isn't their owner** can be easily corrected by a swiftly delivered **kick to the testicles**.

Whether riding a chestnut mare around a private equestrian centre or having a fun bet of a few thousand 'squids' on a 10–1 outsider at Leopardstown, South Dubliners have always had a special affinity with **horses**. Of course, as they're descendants of Ireland's landed gentry, that's perhaps not so surprising. South Dublin girls generally receive their first **pony** at the age

SSIAs

The so-called miracle boom in Ireland's economy, which began in the late 1990s, left a nation once accustomed to being skint in the unusual position of having money for the first time in their lives. In May 2001, concerned that many Southsiders were squandering this new-found wealth on hot tubs, pool tables, decking and swimming pools, the government introduced the SSIA, a special savings investment scheme that promised savers €1 for every €4 they put away each month, provided they left the money untouched for a period of five years. These accounts reached maturity between the spring of 2006 and the spring of 2007, with hundreds of thousands of people collecting lump sums of up to five figures.

Most then squandered this money on hot tubs, pool tables, decking and swimming pools.

of **seven or eight**, and it usually remains their favourite thing in the world until they get their first **Mini Cooper** or **Volkswagen Beetle** at the age of seventeen.

South Dubliners are a famously **green-fingered** lot. Most Saturday and Sunday afternoons they can be found perusing the aisles in one of the area's several hundred **garden centres**, or looking on as some Lithuanian called Szolt mows their lawn or powerhoses their decking. Due to its hot climate, South Dublin is home to a large number of exotic plants, trees and flowers not found anywhere else in Western Europe. Beautifully coloured **orchids** grow in abundance, flowering at all times of the year. Palm trees, which usually survive only in the tropical latitudes between 23.5°N and 23.5°S, thrive and abound and you'll find more palm species here than in Madagascar.

You can walk down most streets, pick a fresh **mango**, **guava** or **coconut** from a tree and eat it – though few South Dubliners do, as they're available in **Superquinn** for as little as a few euro.

Architecture

South Dubliners are known the world over for their impeccable taste in architecture and the region boasts some of the most exquisite buildings in Europe.

The **Radisson SAS St Helen's Hotel** in Booterstown is the place where magnificent Georgian splendour meets glass. St Helen's House was built around the mid eighteenth century and was home to a great many top knobs. Lovingly restored by one of the world's best-known hotel chains, and with two giant, three-storey steel-and-glass wings added to either side, it's now a luxury hotel where you can eat asparagus and truffle scent – just like the top knobs of yesteryear.

Take a sliproad off the M50 motorway and you can experience something like the wonder that Marco Polo felt when he first arrived at the court of Kubla Khan. **Dundrum Town Centre** is a shopping Xanadu, almost 100,000,000 sq. ft of brick and Perspex, housing South Dublin's biggest retail Pleasuredome.

The magnificent **Blackrock Clinic** on the Rock Road could be best described as a six-star luxury hotel that just happens to carry out operations. The building's grey façade, which has been likened to something from the Soviet era, belies its breathtaking interior, the centrepiece of which is a 30-ft waterfall in the central atrium, around which toucans, parakeets, macaws and birds of paradise fossick gaily. At the same time, the soft, playful music of the pan pipes acts as balm for your mind as you're wheeled into theatre to have your cataracts removed, or your vasectomy reversed. Provided, that is, that you are a private, or VHI-positive, patient.

The all-new **Killiney Dart Station** is where public service mass-transportation meets concept art. Damien Hirst is rumoured to be among its admirers, the man who once sawed a cow in half, put it in formaldehyde and got called a genius. The new design, which was completed in 2006, was inspired by movies such as *Battlestar Galactica* and *2001: A Space Odyssey,* and few would disagree that this enormous tubular steel and plate-glass structure greatly enhances the view of Killiney Bay. An interesting piece of trivia is that, along with the Great Wall of China, it's one of only two man-made structures in the world that are visible from space.

South Dublin Homes

South Dubliners love their homes, which explains why so many of them own two or three. It also explains why people come from all over the world to marvel at their splendour. South Dublin houses are famous for combining contemporary architecture with historical building styles in a manner that's very tasteful. Here are some of the most celebrated types:

Mock-Tudor is an imitation of a style that first became popular in England during the reign of Henry VIII. Its most distinctive feature is its black-and-white, half-timber design. This style, also known as Tudorbethan, became popular again in the twentieth century in a number of former British colonies, especially those that maintained an emotional attachment to the Crown. There are hundreds of examples of Mock-Tudor houses in Foxrock and Dublin 4.

Difficult as it is to believe as you're gazing in wonder at the turrets, pointed arches and flying buttresses of

Killiney's skyline, Gothic was a pejorative term used by Renaissance critics to deride the architectural style's deviation from Classical Greek and Roman precepts. In this case, Gothic meant Barbarian. How times have changed! Nowadays, **Mock-Gothic**, which was born out of an eighteenth- and nineteenth-century revival, is South Dublin's most romantic architectural style, as well as its most popular, implying, as it does, an ancient yet

A WORD FROM FIONN

South Dublin is home to a number of buildings of historic and architectural interest – and not all of them have been razed to make way for shopping centres.

Personally, I love Monkstown Parish Church, a huge structure that was built, if memory serves, in 1832 and which dominates the centre of the village. It's amazing that thousands of people pass by it on the bus every day and don't give it so much as a glance. Of course, it's had its critics over the years. Weston St John Joyce described it as a 'nondescript structure that disfigures its site', and Dr Richard Brooke, its first incumbent, said it was, 'large and gaunt and lofty and ugly – a satire on taste, a libel on all ecclesiastical rule, mocking at proportion and symmetry'.

Which is interesting . . .

entirely spurious lineage. A Mock-Gothic house in Killiney – complete with imitation pointed towers, ribbed vaults and clerestory stained-glass windows – would set you back €25 million, which just goes to show that those Renaissance critics weren't half as clever as Sherry FitzGerald.

Most of the new mansions being built for South Dublin's *arrivistes* are **Mock-Georgian**, a style characterized by its rational sense of symmetry and proportion. Features to look out for include the large, vertical sash-and-bay windows, sober grey stone frontage and heavy wooden doors with round-headed windows above, which were first in vogue during the reign of the Georges in the eighteenth and early nineteenth centuries.

Education 🍎

You've been to the doctor and it's confirmed – fertilization has occurred. What do you do next? Call your partner, then your mother, or perhaps a friend to share the news? Head straight to Mothercare to buy a babygro as a visualization exercise? Draw up plans to convert the spare room into a nursery? Not if you're from South Dublin, where the first imperative for all parents-to-be is to get the little one's name down on the waiting list for one of the area's **elite, fee-paying**

schools. To outsiders, this might seem a tad premature. But remember, once the male sperm cell has fused with the female *ovum*, the baby is already a **zygote** – the stage of pregnancy that occurs thirteen or fourteen years before the child enters the second level of the education system. For South Dubliners, that's barely enough time to get them on the register of a prestigious institute of learning. In fact, a number of these schools now request prospective parents to undergo a standard pregnancy test in their presence before agreeing to enroll their unborn child in the school.

South Dublin children are the most expensively educated students in the world. So seriously do their parents regard education that many are prepared to send their little ones to **schools outside of South Dublin** to ensure they get the best advantages.

Finding the best school for their child is an obsession with most Southside couples from as early as the 'trying for a baby' stage of pregnancy. Many parents consider league tables to be an accurate index of the quality of a school, while others go with their lifelong allegiance to their own *alma mater*.

The best schools for boys, in no particular order of preference, are: **Blackrock College**, St Michael's, St Mary's College, Terenure College, Castleknock College, Clongowes Wood, Newbridge College, St Andrew's and St Columba's. For girls it simply must be one of the following: **Mount Anville**, and then Loreto on the Green, Holy Child Killiney, Loreto Foxrock, Alexandra College, Muckross, Loreto Dalkey and Rathdown.

The exam that goes a long way towards defining the course of many Southsiders' lives comes at the end of their final year in secondary school. The **Leaving Certificate** is essentially a memory test. Students spend two months of their final school year reading past exam papers in an effort to anticipate what questions might be asked in each subject by trying to discern the pattern in which topics have come up in the past. They then memorize pages and pages of information they don't necessarily understand, using various retention techniques, such as mnemonics. This information is then regurgitated onto a page during the course of the exam, and forgotten within minutes of the student leaving the exam hall.

Even stupid kids who can't manage this simple mental exercise aren't without hope. South Dublin has a large number of **grind schools** that will drill into a child's head the causes of the Franco-Prussian War, the difference between a Shakespearean and a Petrarchan sonnet, and the principles of trigonometry – for a fee equivalent to that of maintaining **gambling and crack cocaine addictions for a year**.

South Dublin is the site of Ireland's two most famous **third-level institutions**, namely UCD (University

College Dublin) and DBS (Dublin Business School). There's also TCD (Trinity College Dublin), one of South Dublin's premier tourist attractions, where the Book of Kells is housed. It offers classes in a number of subjects.

Young people in South Dublin have more educational opportunities than their contemporaries anywhere else in the world. There are a large number of **private third-level colleges** where you don't need to have your Leaving Cert. – or even an ability to **write your own name** – in order to be accepted. These centres of academic excellence offer degrees and similar equivalents from such prestigious institutes of learning as the University of Bishkek, the Advanced Technical Institute of Maseru and the College of Marketing and Legal Studies in Bandar Seri Begawan. Many South Dubliners are pleasantly surprised to discover that these qualifications are recognized by **their fathers' companies** or their **fathers' friends' companies**, where many of them will spend the rest of their working lives.

National Service

Unlike young people in many European countries, South Dubliners are not required to serve a period in military service. However, at some point in either their late teens or early twenties they are required by law to go to **Australia** for a year. The majority of Southsiders choose to undertake this obligation immediately after finishing third-level college. It's often referred to as 'taking a year oush' or 'doing a bit of travelling', though in truth they will spend an average of ten of their twelve months in Bondi, a suburb in Sydney that has been nicknamed 'County Bondi' because of the way it has been colonized by the Irish. The rest of the time these young people will spend 'doing Cairns', which means learning how to surf, paraglide, abseil, pothole, bungee jump, scuba dive – and have intercourse with other backpackers in several different languages.

It's not all adventure sports, binge-drinking and indiscriminate sex, of course. There is also a **serious, educational dimension** to 'doing the whole Australia thing'.

Many who make the trip are keen to discover once and for all whether the water does in fact flush down the toilet in the opposite direction in the Southern Hemisphere. Others will gain a keen insight into Far Eastern culture when they visit a tattoo parlour in King's Cross and have some Chinese letters inked onto their arm or leg as a permanent reminder of their visit to a city that's 3,500 miles away from Beijing. And just about everybody under the age of twenty-five who goes to Australia learns how to receive money from their parents through **Western Union** – the most important life skill many of them will ever need.

Sports "O

Rugby

There's little Southsiders enjoy more than their rugby, and every year a team called **Leinster** represents South Dublin in the **Heineken Cup**. With star performers such as **Brian O'Driscoll**, **Gordon D'Arcy** and **Shane Horgan**, Leinster is Europe's most glamorous team, though their tendency to underperform on the big occasions has led supporters of their great rivals, Munster, to christen them **'Ladyboys'**. In Munster, a ladyboy is anyone who washes his hands after **having a piss**.

Munster fans are known the world over for their passion and for the high-decibel support that has turned their base of Thomond Park into a fortress. Leinster fans take a different tack and try to unnerve visiting teams by feigning disinterest and remaining deathly silent throughout matches. Facing the famous **Ballsbridge Hush** is said to be one of the most intimidating experiences in sport. On the rare occasions that they are moved to sing, it's a rousing chorus of 'Allez les Bleus', a song that reflects the fact that many Leinster fans have **second homes** in the South of France.

Leinster supporters also have a sense of style and

flamboyance that matches that of their team. At games, most prefer to wear the team's **alternative strip**, which is comprised of a pink shirt and blond streaks in their hair, with designer shades worn on top of the head. For the women it's UGG boots, mini-skirts and tops that expose at least six inches of midriff. As the early rounds of the Heineken Cup take place during the **winter months**, the St John's ambulance service generally has extra crews on hand at matches to deal with cases of **frostbite and hypothermia**.

The anthem of Munster's supporters is 'The Fields of Athenry', a song that has a special resonance for tens of thousands of Limerick people because it's about a petty thief. The song is set in the West of Ireland around the time of the Famine (1845–9). Recently it has been suggested that a new version be written to place it in a more modern context, with Michael stealing not Trevellion's corn but his iPod, then being shot dead in a feud with a rival Limerick family.

The Leinster Schools Senior Cup
The Leinster Schools Senior Cup has long since replaced the Leaving Certificate as *the* defining event in the lives of young South Dublin males. Success or failure in

the famous knockout competition – dominated for a century and a quarter by the elite, fee-paying schools – marks students down as **winners or losers** in the eyes of their peers . . . for ever.

Despite his phenomenal success as a rugby player, captain of industry and philanthropist, **Sir Anthony O'Reilly** is perhaps best known for having never won the Leinster Schools Senior Cup with Northside school **Belvedere**. And even though he captained both Ireland and the Lions, **Brian O'Driscoll** will never live down the shame of his Blackrock College team being knocked out at the semi-final stage in 1998.

Notwithstanding that notable defeat, his *alma mater* has won the competition sixty-five times, which is **more than all the other winners put together**.

The Cup traditionally kicks off in January and culminates with a final played at Lansdowne Road, usually on St Patrick's Day and attended by as many as 25,000 people, almost all of them girls wearing mini-skirts that wouldn't cover the palm of your hand. Many of them later **throw themselves** at members of the winning team at the end of a **marathon, under-age alco-pops binge**. It is estimated that thousands of criminally ugly teenage boys who might otherwise have died virgins have experienced intimacy with beautiful girls thanks to their abilities with a rugby ball.

In many schools being on the 'S', that is the Senior Cup team, is sufficient to exempt a student from studies and, beyond school, from doing **anything else with his life**. The Cup is usually presented to the victors by the mother of the winning captain. If, as often happens, she is a **yummy-mummy**, she is in danger of being crushed in a stampede of adolescent boys, eager to collect their medals and cop a **sly grope** during the congratulatory kiss.

A WORD FROM ROSS

I've got something here around my neck, roysh, that Brian O'Driscoll will never have – a Leinster Schools Senior Cup winner's medal. We actually won it in, like, 1999, beating Newbridge in the final, a bunch of boggers it has to be said. Of course, Drico's probably too old to repeat now, which I happen to know eats him up inside.

Hockey

In South Dublin's elite girls' schools, hockey is the equivalent of rugby – in other words it is generally played by **ugly kids** who sweat a lot. Hockey is an exciting sport, but sadly its growth has been stymied by its high post-school dropout rate and its image as a game for women who like their hair short and spiky, listen to Joni Mitchell and can **change a tyre**. As a general rule, girls tend to give up hockey when they discover boys. Girls who discover girls continue playing, and all efforts to make it sexier, including making the **skirts shorter**, seem doomed to failure.

In 2005 South Dublin was the venue for the women's hockey **World Cup**. Thousands of men flocked to **Belfield** to check out whether foreign players were easier on the eye than their own. They quickly flocked out again.

Golf

Golf provides a vital staple of conversation between males who would otherwise have nothing to say to one another. You'll often hear South Dublin 'men of a certain age' engage in **friendly banter and good-natured raillery** about that skewed drive off the third tee that everyone out in Portmarnock remembers so well, or that putt from 30 ft in Elm Park that owed more to luck than anything else.

Golf is no longer an elitist game. In fact it's the most popular sport among Dublin taxi drivers, though the good news is that you can still play a round of golf without running into one. Thankfully, in South Dublin the old traditions are still very much alive.

Many South Dublin men are members of the K Club, the venue for the 2006 Ryder Cup, which was originally built for golfers who couldn't get into Elm Park or Milltown, South Dublin's super-exclusive clubs **(see page 163)**. Membership of a decent golf club can set

you back up to €40,000 per year, though money isn't the biggest issue. When you apply to join you are entering a world of Byzantine politics, which involves enormous amounts of networking and shameless cosying up to some of the **biggest arses you've ever had the displeasure to meet**. In other words, it's just like a career at the bar. It's no coincidence that 40 per cent of all golf club memberships in South Dublin are held by members of the **legal profession**.

Unfortunately, in recent years almost all golf clubs have been forced to accept **ladies** as members.

A WORD FROM OISINN

Some of the richest men in Ireland, we're talking billionaire property developers here, would give up half their fortunes to get their hands on what I have: membership of Elm Park Golf Club. Yeah, I'm out there every Saturday morning, tramping the fairways with the great and the good, we're talking surgeons, judges and government ministers. You want to know the funniest thing about that? I can't even hit a focking ball straight. The reason I got in is because my old man is a member, and he had my name down before they'd cut my focking umbilical cord. So all these goys with their new money, if they wanted to play Elm Park, I'd have to sign them in!

Royal Dublin Horse Show

One of the **world's premier equestrian events** takes place in South Dublin over the course of five days in early August. The centrepiece of the Royal Dublin Horse

Show is the famous Aga Khan Cup, though the event is as much a **social occasion** as a sporting one, drawing upwards of 20,000 spectators to the **RDS** in Ballsbridge.

A WORD FROM ROSS

It's a little-known fact, roysh, but the Horse Show is basically the best week of the year for getting your Nat King in Dublin. Horsy birds are always gagging for it, as everyone knows. But Protestant horsy birds from the country – they can never get enough.

Anyway, roysh, come the middle of August it's not difficult to find a bird who's ticking all those boxes around Ballsbridge. During the week of the horse show, roysh, Old Belvedere opens up its ground on Anglesea Road as a car park. Or is it the other way around? Maybe it's a car park that Old Belvedere opens up eleven months of the year to allow people to play rugby very badly – basically it's one of those half-empty or half-full questions. Anyway, roysh, my point is that the place ends up being wall-to-wall – or sideline-to-sideline – with man-hungry Proddy boggers with trailers. Honestly, roysh, I've slept in hay more nights than *Moscow Flier*.

Interestingly, it is believed to be the only event that has South Dublin's elite rubbing padded shoulders with country people, or **'boggers'**.

The most colourful day of the week is undoubtedly Ladies' Day, when rich women don summer frocks, high heels and wide-brimmed hats, drink Pimms and Champagne, and complain among themselves about the awful smell of the horses **and the country people**.

Sailing

For many South Dubliners, there's no better way to rid yourself of the stresses of a week stuck in a big car on a gridlocked road than spending Saturday and Sunday stuck in a big boat on the gridlocked **Irish Sea**. The coast between Blackrock and Sandycove is often referred to as the **Irish Riviera**. When the Champagne is flowing aboard the 100-ft Sunseekers and Wally Yachts berthed in sun-drenched Dún Laoghaire harbour, it's difficult to believe you're not in Monte Carlo.

The attraction to sailing is more social than sporting, and most of those who would identify themselves as **'Yachties'** have, in fact, never set foot on a boat that wasn't anchored firmly to the seabed. The people who do leave the harbour can be broken down into two sub-groups: sailors and motorboaters. The former tend to look down on the latter – and the rest of the world. **Sailors** are usually wealthy professional types, such as doctors and barristers, who don't mind getting their hair wet or the clatter of a boom. To **motorboaters**, sailing involves simply turning the ignition switch in their Gin Palaces, or Stink Pots – so called because of their foul-smelling diesel engines. They tend to avoid any sea conditions that might cause them to spill their **Mount Gay tonics**.

Yachties have their own **style of dress**, which has now crossed over into mainstream fashion. It was they who first made Dubes popular, although they refer to them as **'Dockies'**. **Beige canvas trousers** and **Henri-Lloyd weatherproof jackets** were also part of the sailing look before being appropriated by a generation of rugby types.

Sailing also has its own version of rugger-huggers – in the form of simpering bimbos who chase sailors around like a bunch of **boy-band groupies**. They're known as **Dockside Dollies** or, in the case of the big game hunters, **Racer Chasers**. They tend to wear Gucci clothes that never see so much as a splash of salt water, perch sunglasses on top of their heads and generally act like they're aboard a 120-ft Hinckley in Cape Cod.

Skiing

Despite enjoying a subtropical climate all year round, Southsiders take to the snow like **Chukchi Eskimos**. Every year tens of thousands of them migrate to the Alps to spend a fortnight hurtling down mountainsides at 90 mph on two narrow slats of fibreglass. Skiing holidays are regarded as an indicator of status in South Dublin; where you choose to go is considered an accurate barometer of your social standing. The super-rich gravitate towards **Meribel**, **Val d'Isere** and **Verbier** – or 'Verbs', as it's more commonly known – while **Andorra** and **Bulgaria** tend to attract people who were born working class but have been processed into middle class by the upturn in the Irish economy – the so-called **new *faux riche***.

Like golf, skiing has its own rituals and codes of behaviour. Women, for instance, tend to go to **Pamela Scott** on Grafton Street and spend thousands of euro on 'off-piste' fashions, while picking up the **cheapest pair of ski boots** they can find in The Great Outdoors – boots that are unlikely ever to leave their box.

Men tend to take the sporting side more seriously and will often be heard trying to outdo each other with their **experience and knowledge** of the world's most famous slopes, saying things like, 'We took the kids to Whistler a couple of years ago and found it about four or five degrees too cold to ski,' or 'St Moritz would be perfect if it weren't so low.'

Most South Dubliners take between two and three ski holidays a year, and hopes are high that the area will one day produce an Olympic champion, that is if **skiing downhill while hungover on Eiswein** ever becomes an Olympic event.

Music

South Dubliners are well known for their appreciation
of music, which is no surprise given that most of them
receive their **first musical instrument** before the
placenta has been washed from their bodies. In fact,
most will have developed an ear for music even before
that as South Dublin mothers, ever keen to impart
culture to their children as early as possible, use
Personal Sound Systems to play classical music to
their babies in the womb. This explains why, by the
time they reach Montessori school, many children can
recognize **Rachmaninov's 'Rhapsody on a Theme
of Paginini'** before basic spelling-aid symbols such as
an apple or a ball.

Nowhere is South Dublin's love affair with music
more in evidence than on Grafton Street on a Saturday
afternoon, when boys and girls in evening dress
demonstrate their wonderful proficiency with various
string and wind instruments.

Technically, they are 'busking', but don't feel under
pressure to give them money – their parents are **rolling
in it**, and they won't starve.

Grafton Street is occasionally the site of other
impromptu musical performances, such as Traveller
children singing 'The Fields of Athenry' using just two

notes, and also Northsiders doing what's known as 'human beat-boxing', but the Gardaí usually **move these people on**.

Given this rich and vibrant musical scene, it's little wonder that South Dublin produced one of the most successful popular music acts in the world right now. **The Thrills** 'broke America' just two years after they formed in 2001 and have since sold hundreds of thousands of records worldwide. Like U2's *The Joshua Tree*, their breakthrough album came at the end of a spiritual and musical journey through the soul of America, though, unlike U2, they were on a **J1er** at the time.

Just like Scottish band The Proclaimers, who resisted pressure from the industry to soften their strong Kilmarnock brogues, Thrills frontman **Conor Deasey** has also refused to compromise his accent on hits such as 'One Horse Town' and 'Big Sur' and continues to sing in a style South Dubliners recognize – that of **Beverly Hills**.

Rugby Songs

Those few South Dubliners without a classical music education can still 'turn a tune' – even if it is a grossly offensive one. Believe it or not, many of the bawdy rugby songs we all love were first improvised in South

Dublin pubs, on buses travelling to and from rugby matches, or on the street in the early hours of the morning! Among the best-known are:

Oh Give Me a Clone
(*to the tune of* Home on the Range)

Oh give me a clone,
Of my own flesh and bone,
With the Y chromosome changed to an X.
Then when it's full-grown,
My own flesh and bone,
Will be of the opposite sex.

Bestiality's Best
(*to the tune of* Tie Me Kangaroo Down, Sport)

Chorus
Bestiality's best, boys,
Bestiality's best (fock a Wallaby),
Bestiality's best, boys,
Bestiality's best.

Stick your lug in a slug, Doug,
Stick your lug in a slug.
Stick your lug in a slug, Doug,
Stick your lug in a slug.

Chorus

Suggested verses:
Stick your pole in a mole, Noel.
Intercourse with a horse, Boris.
Up the rear of a deer, Ciar.
Blow your load in a toad, Maude.
Give some love to a dove, Guv.
Stick your lat in a cat, Matt.

A WORD FROM JP
Many times in the Bible we are told to honour God through music. 'Speak to one another with psalms, hymns and spiritual songs,' the Book of Ephesians tells us. 'Sing and make music in your heart to the Lord, always giving thanks to God the Father for everything, in the name of our Lord Jesus Christ.' Amen to that.

I've always loved music, although these days I'm listening to a lot less Snoop Dogg and 50 Cent and a lot more of Cliff Richard's *Gospel Hits Remastered*.

Religion

See **Rugby**.

Language 🍎

South Dublin is regarded as one of the most difficult languages in the world to master, not least because of the number of age- and gender-specific dialects in common usage. Men speak a version of the language that is only loosely related to that spoken by women, while boys and girls speak two different variations that are barely on nodding terms with one other, although there are of course features common to all four.

In a broad sense, South Dublin is a form of creolized English, a hybrid of the language used by the **British aristocracy** and that spoken by the characters from popular American television programmes, such as *Friends*. The unlikely fusion of the two, essentially hay-nay-brain-cay meets Central Perk, reflects South Dublin's identification with the English upper classes (reinforced by Anglocentric education methods in the elite schools) and its rather shallow efforts to ape the cool, pretty people it sees on television, sitting in comfy, colourful chairs and saying implausibly humorous things to one another while drinking cappuccinos from improbably large cups. Adults tend more towards the former and young people towards the latter, but again the two elements are present to varying degrees in both.

The language is far too complex to enter into any detailed examination in this book. Visitors who want to understand adults would be best advised to read the collected **Jeeves and Wooster** books by P. G. Wodehouse before they travel to South Dublin. To understand young people it might be helpful to watch a DVD box set, or two, of *Dawson's Creek* or *Sex and the City*.

Here are a few general guidelines to get you started:

- The hard 'T' sound in the middle and at the end of almost all words becomes a sibilant 'sh', e.g. trout becomes **troush**, right is **roysh** and marketing is **morkeshing**.

- Linguistic crutches, such as 'like' and 'roysh', are ubiquitous in spoken South Dublin, so be liberal in using them.

- The harsh-sounding 'ar' sound is softened to become 'or'. Thus, harsh becomes **horsh**. Arts is **Orts**. The bar is **the bor**. The car is **the cor**. *The Star* is a **newspaper read by poor people**.

- The 'ow' sound is numbed to sound like 'ay', as in what's known as BBC English. Loud becomes **layd**.

Pound becomes **paynd**. Crowd becomes **crayd**. Roundabout become **rayndabaysh**.

- Young people, in particular, tend to raise the intonation at the very end of their sentences so that statements of fact sound like **questions**. For example, you might overhear a young man tell a friend, breathlessly:

  'I was, like, sitting at the bor? And this, like, total honey came in, wearing, like, pretty much nothing? And she was, like, totally checking me out and shit?'

  This particular inflection is of Australian origin and was adopted into the language of South Dublin thanks to the popularity of television soap operas like *Home and Away* and *Neighbours*. In Australia, it's called the HRTs, or the **High Rise Thermals**.

- In conversational South Dublin, young people also tend towards US vernacular forms of speech attribution, e.g.

  I was like, 'Look at the state of the girl,' and **he was there**, 'I know. She has a face like a bucket of smashed crabs.'

- Another feature, English in origin but now common currency in South Dublin, mixes the singular subject with the plural verb form, e.g. **I goes**, 'She really is sinfully ugly. She looks like her face caught fire and someone put it out with a focking golf shoe,' and **he goes**, 'I know. Why did you marry her then?'

- Young men, in particular, use a lot of cockney-style **rhyming slang**, but with an Irish flavour. **Britneys** are beers (Spears). The **Daniel Day** is the Luas (Daniel Day-Lewis). An **Allied Irish** is an act of self-harm believed to induce hair growth on the palms of one's hands.

(*Note:* some of the more common phrases used in South Dublin are contained in the ThesauRoss at the back of this book.)

 A WORD FROM CHRISTIAN
Did you know there's an actual language called Jawa? I'd like to learn it, even just to have enough to get by, in case ... It's hard to get the tapes, though. The looks they give me in Hughes & Hughes in Dún Laoghaire. I know that *Ootini* means 'Come on' and I know that *hubba gourd* – this, like, fruit they live on – means 'staff of life'. I suppose you'd want to know more than that if you ever found yourself on Tatooine and you needed, like, directions or fuel for your Landspeeder ...

Shopping ♀

South Dublin is a shopper's paradise, a nirvana of consumption, a consumer heaven, where **all major credit cards** are accepted and where being 'maxed to the hilt' is not a dirty expression.

For generations Grafton Street was the most prestigious shopping street in Dublin City Centre. In terms of commercial activity, however, it has been eclipsed in recent years by the Northside's Henry Street, which has been rejuvenated since the opening of the Jervis Shopping Centre and the arrival of marquee high-street names, such as Zara and H&M. At the same time, the only retail growth in the South City Centre is in the area of **mobile phone retailers** and **newsagents**, which have succeeded in attracting an unwelcome number of peasants to what was once the city's most upmarket strip.

Grafton Street may no longer be the wonderland once immortalized in song, but most South Dubliners still find it reassuring to know that there is somewhere they can go on a Saturday afternoon to pick up those essential bits and pieces, such as **fur coats**, **boxes of Havanas** and **Rolex watches**. Best of all, Grafton Street has **Brown Thomas**, the world's smartest department store, where you can buy everything from a

Louis Vuitton handbag for €2,000 to a **Hermès** handbag for €4,000. 'BTs', as it's fondly known to its *habitués*, exudes **class**, from the **commissionaire** who holds open the door, to the stunning **Gráinne Seoige-lookalikes** carrying out extensive plasterwork on the faces of middle-aged posh ladies at the many make-over counters.

Further up the street, the **Powerscourt Townhouse Centre** is a mansion stuffed to the gills with trendy women's fashions, antique jewellery, designer silverware and fine food, which means the people who shop there quite literally feel **right at home**.

Grafton Street has jewellery shops to suit all pockets. **Ernest Jones** has Tag Heuer watches for €2,500, or, if you're in the market for an expensive one, **Weir & Son** has three windows (shatterproof and alarmed) of Rolexes, which average out at about €35,000 apiece. And yes, that is a comma you're staring at, not a decimal point.

If books are your thing and you're looking to get rid of the last of your holiday shrapnel, **Cathach Books** on Duke Street has a first edition of *Finnegans Wake*, signed by **James Joyce**, for €14,000. The shop also stocks a range of collector's editions from **Flann O'Brien** and other famous Irish authors, which couldn't be shifted when they first came out but now sell for as much as the price of a Hermès vanity case.

A visit to Grafton Street wouldn't be complete

without a trip to **Barnardo**, purveyors of **fine furs**. A word of warning: it is not to be confused with Barnardo's, the UK-based charity that cares for vulnerable children and operates a large number of 'op-shops'. While both sell second-hand clothes, in the case of Barnardo the previous owners were foxes and baby seals. If you can brave the occasional **spotty adolescent protester** outside its doors, you can browse through the finest collection of furs in Ireland. And about €5,000 is all it'll cost to kit you out like

DUBES

Docksiders, as the name suggests, started out life as boat shoes, worn by yachtie types. Now, marina chic has crossed over into mainstream fashion and Dubarry's signature leather deck shoes – in either navy or brown – are the most popular choice of footwear for young men and young women in South Dublin. They suit tracksuit bottoms and jeans as well as they do chinos, which is why they're regarded as the anytime shoe. Wear them to the cinema with your sloppy O'Neill's tracksuit bottoms, or to school, or to that all-important job interview – with total confidence. The even better news is that their price tag – €100 a pop – puts them well out of the range of poor people.

A WORD FROM ROSS

Dubes are quite simply the footwear of the gods. I've been wearing them since I was basically ten. But it's, like, SO not cool if you don't know the secret of the perfect deck-shoe knot:

1. Double the lace back on itself.
2. Holding half the length of the double lace together, take the loop end and twist it at least four times around the doubled part.
3. Pass the loose end through the remaining loop.
4. Holding the twists firmly, pull the shoe end of the lace back through the twist until the loop is tight over the loose end.

Easy, huh? And don't forget, I got *nul points* in the old Leaving Cert.

Cruella De Vil. Just think of the looks of horror at your next dinner party when you tell them how many chinchillas had to die to make it!

The suburbs of South Dublin are also crammed with top-quality shops, which are dealt with on a region-by-region basis in the second section of this book.

South Dublin Shop Girls

Despite the region's obscene wealth and prosperity, many teenage girls in South Dublin are forced to **work**. This is sometimes at the behest of socially conscious parents who think it's important for young Sophie or Chloë to learn self-sufficiency and pay for her own UGG boots and Polo Sport Tote handbags. Most of these unfortunates end up working behind the counter in clothes shops or department stores.

South Dublin Shop Girls are famous for their ability to maintain two **conflicting moods** at the same time: one of sulky indifference towards the customer, and one of over-the-top chattiness to a friend, who will be either at the next cash register or on the other end of the mobile phone into which the South Dublin Shop Girl will almost inevitably be talking while serving you. South Dublin Shop Girls believe that working is 'like, SO, below' them and accordingly take it out on the customer, whom they regard with **disinterest**, if not downright **contempt**.

South Dublin Shop Girls speak in a type of codified language that can be difficult to break down, but it's definitely worth learning a few key phrases if you intend going on a shopping trip. If, for example, you hand a South Dublin Shop Girl a €50 note for an item that costs €45.65, you will usually be asked: 'Have you got the sixty-five?' This literally means, 'Despite my expensive private education and Saturday morning maths grinds, I'm too lazy to do even simple arithmetic.'

Occasionally, the size of a particular item you are looking for will not be on display in the shop. You might ask, 'Have you got this in an 8?' and be asked in turn, 'Is there not one out there?' This literally means, 'I am SO not going into that storeroom in these shoes. It's, like, I shouldn't even be here? Oh my God, I SO hate my parents.'

A WORD FROM ROSS
Just a quick word about sizes, roysh. They're totally different in South Dublin than anywhere else in the world, what with Southside girls looking after their figures the way they do. Your dress size might be a size 10 in the real world, but in South Dublin you probably wouldn't get a 10 over your head. As a rule of thumb, remember that Large means emaciated, Medium means skeletal and Small means advanced decomposition.

Food and Drink

Skobies have their curry sauce, culchies have their coleslaw – and South Dubliners have their **sun-dried**

tomatoes. There's far more to the Southside culinary experience than these beguiling and versatile little gems, however, even if they do come with virtually every meal.

It is a little-known fact, for instance, that, per capita, Southsiders eat more **Provolone, Ligurian olives and roast pepper quiche** than any other nation in the world, and that 40 per cent of the world's **smoked salmon terrine with lefse and truffle cream** is consumed here. The truth is that South Dublin is a gastronome's delight, home of the famous **goat's cheese- and prosciutto-stuffed shrimp with tomato and basil couscous**. And where else but in this epicurean heaven could you walk into any streetside café or restaurant and have the chef fix you a chicken, feta and ricotta bake inside a matter of minutes, washed down with a nice bottle of Château Lestage Simon Haut-Médoc 2000?

South Dublin restaurants are well known for their sense of adventure and are not scared to wrap a piece of **Parma ham** around almost anything and charge you an extra €10 for it. Cured meats and soft cheeses are very popular, and takeaway gourmet food emporiums, such as **Donnybrook Fair**, **Cavistons**, **Fallon & Byrne**, **The Unicorn** and **Avoca Handweavers**, cater for the enormous demand for Mediterranean food, helping to bring a little bit of **Puerto Banus** to the Southside suburbs. Italy can claim credit for Parmesan, but South

Dublin invented **Parmesan shavings**, which go with just about everything – at least on one side of the Liffey.

South Dubliners eat more **spinach** in an average year than Popeye, though, interestingly, the cartoon is banned in most homes because of its glorification of **processed food**. In the South Dublin version of the story, the famous sailor gains his strength not by gobbling down a soggy, dark-green, tinned version of the foodstuff but by eating a **spinach, red cabbage and green mango salad** or – when Brutus has really incensed him – some **spinach, carrot and white kidney bean pâté** on warm focaccia.

South Dubliners are unreconstructed snobs when it comes to their food. A pizza is called a *tort*, an omelette is a *frittata*, and trifle is *tiramisu*. Play it safe and order a traditional Irish breakfast and you can be assured that the sausages will come spiced with **tomatoes and olives**. Say the word **'rocket'** to your average South Dubliner and he will think not of a vehicle or device propelled by the ejection of fast-moving gas from within its engine but of a leaf vegetable that is an essential ingredient in any salad.

Eating out

When it comes to food, there's only one thing South Dublin men enjoy more than steak and chips – and that's **steak and chips that cost a fortune**. **Shanahan's**, on St Stephen's Green, is where you'll find Ireland's property developers, currency traders and captains of industry loosening their belt buckles a couple of notches and tucking into enormous Angus steaks that resemble a wildebeest with its head and legs chopped off. As a novelty, working-class staples such as onion rings and sautéed mushrooms are given the Shanahan's treatment – served on the finest bone china and with an eye-watering price tag.

The name Patrick Guilbaud is synonymous with fine French cuisine, and **Restaurant Patrick Guilbaud**, in the Merrion Hotel on Merrion Street – 'RPG's', or simply 'Patrick's' to regulars – is the perfect riposte to those who say you can't get a decent *moûles à la crème de Pernod* or *carré d'agneau aux pistaches* in this town any more. The food, like its millionaire clientele, is dressed to impress, and the *entrées* are such works of art that you will feel less of an urge to eat them than to photograph them. The dining experience is enhanced by those little bourgeois **affectations** – forks placed tines-down on the table – that are so loved by South Dublin's modern-day aristos.

Thornton's at the Fitzwilliam Hotel, St Stephen's Green, has stars coming out of its ears – not only Michelin ones but C-list ones, too, all hoping to be spotted eating starters of soufflé of sole and crab with red chard, chive and cream sauce for €30 a pop.

Il Primo on Montague Street is a modest little trattoria whose clientele are typically builders and stockbrokers who fancy a change from Shanahan's, but don't mind paying Shanahan's prices for pasta.

With its modern art, mirrored dining room and European dishes with a subtle Eastern twist, **La Stampa** on Dawson Street is still *the* place for up-and-coming celebrities, media types and movers-and-shakers. Those who say it's a triumph of image over substance might be surprised to know that **Louis Walsh** eats there regularly.

If you are in advertising or public relations, or you are a solicitor with one of Ireland's 'Big Five' firms, then it's likely **The Unicorn** on Merrion Court is your favourite restaurant. Sit back, observe the **air-kissing, back-stabbing and unashamed insincerity** of the clientele as careers are made and broken over farfale with duck and truffle oil and *linguine con polpette*.

Ely Wine Bar on Ely Place is a London yuppie era-style gastro-wine-bar where you'll find the fun crowd from financial services – the so-called **Nerd Herd**. **Town Bar and Grill** on Kildare Street has been called the Treasury Holdings Staff Canteen, but its grilled sardines and clam linguine attract a wide range of very, very interesting people, **from TDs to barristers**. On an average Friday night, **Bang Café** on Merrion Row will have more beautiful people on its books than Giorgio Armani.

If you are a minor celeb who enjoys spotting other minor celebs, then the chances are you are no stranger to the black Dover sole on the bone with saffron, caper and shrimp butter in **Peploe's** on Stephen's Green, while **Bleu Bistro Moderne** on Dawson Street caters specifically for yummy-mummies who drive Volvo XC90s.

A WORD FROM ROSS

If you asked me for my favourite place to bring a bird with a view to, like, getting her in the sack later on, I'd say somewhere like Guilbaud's, or Peploe's, or La Stampa. The problem is that Sorcha's old man goes to those places and Shanahan's and Thornton's are out of bounds as well because my old man goes there, the dickhead. Anyway, roysh, I've discovered this place, L'Gueuleton, which is this, like, bistro on Fade Street, of all places. Great focking nosebag, which explains why people are queuing down the street to try to get a table. See, birds love French nosh. I always have the snails. They're an actual aphrodisiac. Although I had a dozen there recently and one of them didn't work.

Pubs and Clubs

Renard's

Women once outnumbered men by a ratio of 3:1 in here on most Friday and Saturday nights. You know what happens next. The men got word of it, and now men outnumber women to the point where it looks like a gay bar. It's still the place to be seen in Dublin, though. Not that you are guaranteed to be seen at all, of course. Someone apparently eyeing you up is more likely to be admiring him- or herself in one of the club's many floor-to-ceiling mirrors. Don't be put off by the members-only vibe at the door – it's part of its shtick. If you're 'someone', you'll be admitted upstairs to the private club, where you could find yourself playing pool with Val Kilmer, Brian O'Driscoll, Colin Farrell or any of the stars who regularly drop by when they're in town. Great music, delicious cocktails and wall-to-wall eye candy have made Renard's the most South Dublin club in, well, South Dublin.

Lillie's Bordello

The drink is expensive, the dance-floor resembles a squash court and the average punter has an IQ to match his Ralph Lauren collar size. In other words, this is a great Southside club. Guys called Tiernan and

Trevor come here in their designer threads to make bold but vain efforts to click with stuck-up, emaciated South Dublin princesses who have neither personalities nor a sense of humour. Lillie's reputation as *the* place to be on a Friday or Saturday night had as much to do with its officious door policy as its status as an international celebrity hangout. Bono, Mick Jagger, David Beckham, Paul McCartney and Jack Nicholson all show their faces in here when they're in town. You won't get near them, though. The club operates a type of complex caste system: ordinaries are admitted to the first floor; B-list celebs and those on air-kissing terms with the bouncers are granted access to the second floor; while the private tables in the Library at the top of the building are reserved for the Champagne-swilling stars of the social pages. However, talking your way past the bouncers is no longer the job it once was, and, accordingly, Lillie's stock has fallen in recent times as the big spenders desert it for Renard's. Its current regulars are mostly hair stylists and River Island staff.

Ron Black's

With its high ceilings, marble bar counters, dark-wood-panelled walls and off-white furnishings, Ron Black's on Dawson Street resembles London or New York at the height of the 1980s yuppie boom. The main bar gets very crowded on Friday and Saturday nights, but the atmosphere is never unpleasant – it's rather like being trapped in a lift with a bunch of models. They drink Champagne in here like it comes out of the tap. The regular crowd are thirty-something professionals, posers who've never had time for a relationship and gangs of girls on a night out.

Café en Seine

For years Café en Seine was a pub out of its time; it was Celtic Tiger years before there was a Tiger. In 2002 it was given an opulent, Art Deco make-over with a *fin-de-siècle* French theme. The regulars took one look at the Louis XIVth bust, the French hotel lift, grand piano, brass chandeliers and the glass atrium filled with 40-ft trees and rechristened it Café Insane. It was like going on the piss in the Louvre. The management stuck with that Continental café style, and the sound of ringing tills seven days and nights a week explains why it's now referred to simply as Seine. Southsiders love it for its *faux* sophistication, extortionate prices and clientele who are not so much the bold and the beautiful as the vain and the vacuous. A great spot.

Ba Mizu

A river runs through it – quite literally, actually. The River Poddle, a tributary of the Liffey, flows underneath this trendy pub at the back of the Powerscourt Townhouse Shopping Centre and is visible through a series of glass panels set into the floor. There's a lot more to ogle than that, though. Fitted out in dark pine and stone, with plenty of dimly lit, private snugs in which to hide, 'Miz' is stacked wall to wall with ridiculously good-looking after-work types.

Cocoon

The former Formula One star Eddie Irvine owns this place, and it's just a shame it contains nothing of his stellar charisma. The door policy tends to favour beauty over brains, cut-glass accents over personality and smart-casual dress to the exclusion of just about any other look. The result is possibly the most uptight bar in town, where beautiful strangers gather to studiously ignore each other. The women – mainly hair stylists from Toni & Guy – strut around with sulky pouts they imagine look good against the killer background rock score. The men stare at them with the intensity of serial killers, admiring them but not wanting to give them the pleasure of being chatted up. The music might be the best available anywhere in Dublin, but this is a pub that needs a stiff drink and a good seeing-to.

The Bailey

Sink a Slow Cosmopolitan and see the new, flush Ireland reflected in chrome and glass. The Bailey is a paradise for Prada-clad poseurs. Even the legal and financial investment types who pack the place out on a Friday night are refreshingly superficial. On summer evenings the crowd tends to spill out onto South William Street with their drinks, and the obnoxious laughter can be heard as far away as Grafton Street. On Saturdays it tends to attract a transient professional crowd, enjoying whistle-stop cocktails on the way to somewhere even more expensive.

Dakota Bar

This place gets as full and sweaty as a cattle truck, but the ambience, the decorative lounge staff and the uncharacteristically friendly crowd of Southsiders it attracts make the cowpen atmosphere more than bearable. With its great music and personable clientele, Dakota lacks the sterility and soullessness it would need to be taken to many South Dublin hearts, but nonetheless it remains one of the best venues in town to chat up good-looking birds. A word of warning, though: the women in here tend to be smart, many of them Arts students, so you might need more than your usual grab-bag of chat-up lines, such as: 'Do you sleep on your stomach? Can I?'

SPY

The Passionfruit Martinis and the pulsating R 'n' B, funk and jazz tunes are just two of the reasons this club has become so popular; the fact that Justin Timberlake once appeared here are most of the others. The door staff will extend you a traditional South Dublin welcome, in other words they'll tell you they don't know your face, but will eventually let you in, once they've established that you're not muck. The décor is impressive, from the stone entrance archway originally designed for coaches to the high ceilings and chandeliers. The music is excellent, the prices reassuringly expensive and the clientele impervious to your chatter unless you happen to drive a Ferrari.

The Morrison Hotel

What do you do if you want to build a shrine to that very South Dublin notion that image and appearance are everything? Easy – you have one of the world's most famous couturiers plan it for you. John Rocha designed this Arctic-cool hotel bar, taking unfussy minimalism as his motivation and his muse. If Ikea fitted out airport lounges, they would look and feel a lot like this. Dark-oak furnishings and cream leather sofas make it the ideal place to read *The Irish Times* property supplement during the day, and at night to pull a woman who works in '**morkeshing**'.

Searson's

One of the few pubs in South Dublin that hasn't disappeared up its own 'orse', and yet many locals are prepared to forgive it. Its location on Baggot Street – a brisk walk away from Lansdowne Road – has made it a popular hangout for rugby types who want to avoid the stuffiness of other, traditional match-day venues. Searson's has steadfastly resisted the temptation to go trendy or morph into a superpub. 'What's a nice pub like you doing in a place like this?' you might ask.

A WORD FROM ROSS

Want to know how we Celtic Tiger cubs are slaking our thirst of a Friday evening? With the most expensive cocktail in Ireland, of course. It's called Minted and you get them in the Mint Bor in the Westin on, like, Westmoreland Street. It's basically a Vanilla-chocolate Martini, roysh, that's made from vanilla-infused vodka, 200-year-old cognac and actual flakes of, like, 23-carat gold. It's served in a glass of designer crystal, with chocolate truffles on the side.

How much does a Minted cost? Well, if you have to ask, you can't afford one. But, since you did, we're talking €500 each. Basically, if a bird asks you for one of them, you'd want a signed guarantee of your Nat King first.

THE LOCAL DROP

Heino. Ken. Special K. Whatever you choose to call it, there's no disputing that Heineken is South Dublin's favourite drink, enjoyed by everyone from groups of goys watching the rugby in Kielys of Donnybrook to groups of goys on the 'total lash' in Ron Black's or Café en Seine.

Heineken is a pale lager that contains hops, yeast and barley, and is 5 per cent alcohol by volume. What may come as a surprise to many is that this delicious drink originates not in South Dublin but in Holland, where the original Heineken Brewery (Heineken Brouwerijen) was established by Gerard Adriaan Heineken in 1863. Today, the company brews 121.8 million hectolitres of beer per year, most of which will eventually be drunk in South Dublin.

For its sheer enterprise, the Heineken company is a role model for Ireland's young go-getter generation, who always have one eye on the main chance. When Prohibition was ended in America, the first shipment of beer landed legally on its shores came from Heineken – just seventy-two hours after the law was repealed.

In more recent times the company has changed the traditional Heineken logo, considering the old design too formal for its 'big fun' beer. A decision was taken to tilt the three Es in the company name approximately 10° to the left, to make it look like the letters were laughing. There is no evidence to suggest this move has resulted in increased sales, but it did persuade an entire generation of young South Dubliners that there was easy money to be made in 'morkeshing'.

A WORD FROM OISINN

What is the deal with birds and cocktails? As in, why do they only want them when you're getting the round in? Seriously, when they're paying it's like, 'just a Bacordi Breezer', or 'just a vodka and slimline tonic'. When you're paying they're suddenly reaching for the menu and a focking world of choice is opening up in front of them.

I took this bird, Muireann, out a while back. She looked like Joey out of *Dawson's Creek*, no, sorry, Joey out of *Friends*. She's basically an ugly girl who'd make a good-looking bloke, we're talking really offensive-looking, in other words, right up my street.

So I take her to the Ice Bar in the Four Seasons Hotel, obviously trying to impress her. We sit in a quiet corner and she makes a grab for the cocktail menu and the next thing I know she's running her finger down the list, looking for the most expensive one. Anyway, she asks for a Top Shelf Mojito, which was nearly fifteen bills, then switches to Sunburn Martinis because she was a focking fiend for the Stoli. Then she works her way through, in the following order, a Singapore Sling, a Mangotini, a Razmopolitan, a Cosmopolitan, a Raspberry Russian and a D4 Swinger – and I swear to God, not one of those focking drinks touched the side of her throat on the way down. I'm not scabby or anything, but this is at, like, €12.50 a pop.

Eventually, her bladder's crying for mercy and she focks off to the TK Maxx, after telling me to get her another drink while she was gone.

'What do you want?' I said, bracing myself.

'A cocktail,' she said. 'Surprise me.'

So I did. I got her a prawn cocktail, with Marie Rose horseradish sauce. It was there waiting for her when she came back from the can. I wasn't.

Coffee

The Irish are known the world over as a nation of tea-drinkers. Difficult as it is to believe now, twenty years ago there were only **two types** of coffee available in Ireland – **instant or none at all**. Now the country is awash with speciality coffee houses, where you can kick back in a **big, comfy leather armchair** and enjoy a grande skinny no-fun latte, or just the **guilty indulgence** of ordering five cappuccinos while a long queue of people waits to be served, then paying for them with a credit card.

For centuries coffee has oiled the **wheels of revolution** across the globe. The **Boston Tea Party** was planned at the Green Dragon coffee house, and it was at the Café Foy in Paris that Desmoulins jumped on top of a table and whipped the crowd into the revolutionary froth that resulted in the **storming of the Bastille** two days later. In Argentina, the **overthrow of military juntas** has been plotted over double-strength espressos in the famous Café Tortoni in Buenos Aires. **Napoleon** extolled the joys of black coffee and the 'unusual force' it gave him, while **Beethoven**, **Göethe** and **Balzac** found it an indispensable aid to creativity.

Coffee has a long history of inciting passion and stimulating creativity, and in much the same tradition South Dubliners will often be seen whiling away an afternoon over a grande white chocolate mocha or a medio decaf Americano with whip, and engaging in loud discussions about the volume of **traffic** on the Rock Road, or how much their houses have increased in value in the time it's taken their coffee to cool, or even pointlessly tapping the keys of an **iBook**.

Coffee is a language unto itself, and visitors should make sure to learn at least a few phrases. If, for instance, someone asked you for a **tall skinny sleeper with whip**, would you return with a six foot three, underweight Al Qaeda operative with an S&M fetish instead of a decaf latte with two shots of espresso, low-fat milk and whipped cream? It's a more common mistake than you might imagine.

In a few short years, coffee has succeeded in turning the English language on its head. Most **baristas** – or professional 'coffee chefs' – speak a kind of American **corporate patois** that is almost impossible to understand. Adding to the confusion is the fact that most of the big coffee chains have their own exclusive vocabulary. Ask for a harmless split wet mocca with wings in Starbucks, for instance, and you'll be met either by a blank look from the barista or by a member of the shop's **security staff** who will conduct you off the premises.

A Basic Guide to Speaking Coffee

The essential guide below gives you some of the most common words and phrases, what they mean and where they'll be understood.

Phrase	Meaning	Where understood
Americano	An espresso with half a pint of water added to it – especially for Americans who can't take it Italian-style.	Everywhere
Angelico	White chocolate mix with steamed milk, topped with Bourneville chocolate flakes.	Café Java

Phrase	Meaning	Where understood
Brew	Regular, fully brewed coffee.	West Coast Coffee
Caffé	Coffee.	Starbucks
Caffé Misto	Half brewed coffee, half steamed milk.	Starbucks
Cartado	Double espresso with hot milk and foam.	West Coast Coffee
Chiller	An iced cappuccino.	Café Java
Doppio	A double espresso.	Costa
Dry	Extra foam.	Insomnia
Espresso con Panna	Single espresso with whipped cream.	Café Java
Espresso Ice-cap	Iced coffee.	Insomnia
Frap	An ice-blended coffee.	Starbucks
Frappe	An iced coffee.	Café Sol
Frappé	An iced coffee.	West Coast Coffee
Frescato	A type of iced coffee.	Costa
Harmless	Low-fat and decaffeinated.	Insomnia
LightNote	A smooth and delicate blend of coffee with a clean finish.	Starbucks
Macchiato	Foamed milk, espresso, vanilla and buttery caramel.	Starbucks

Phrase	Meaning	Where understood
Mallowchino	Single espresso in a cup filled with cream and steamed milk and topped with marshmallows and Bourneville chocolate flakes.	Café Java
Miscela	An espresso blend with six parts Arabica beans and one part robusta.	Costa
Mollotina	Single espresso mixed with unsweetened chocolate.	Café Java
No fun	Decaffeinated.	Insomnia
Ristretto	A very short, sharp espresso.	Costa
Skinny	Made with low-fat milk.	Insomnia
Split	Half the caffeine.	Insomnia
Tazo	A blend of premium green tea.	Starbucks
Wet	Extra steamed milk.	Insomnia
White Angel	White chocolate with steamed milk.	Insomnia
Wild	With whipped cream.	Insomnia
With Wings	To go.	Insomnia

SIZE DOES MATTER!

One of the most important things to remember when ordering coffee in South Dublin is that there is no equivalent for the word 'small'. Even in a shop where the coffee is served in cups of three equally proportionate sizes, remember you have entered into an Alice in Wonderland world where small is big and big is bloody enormous. If you're ordering a small coffee in Insomnia or West Coast, for instance, you must ask for a tall coffee. In both stores a grande is a large coffee, though a grande is only a medium in Starbucks, where the biggest size is a venti – the Italian word for wheelie bin.

Confused? This short guide to the sizes used by the best-known chains should help you order your coffee successfully, without being reduced to a gibbering wreck or punching the barista in the face:

	Small	*Medium*	*Large*
Starbucks	Tall	Grande	Venti
Café Java	Tall	–	Grande
Café Sol	Short	Tall	Grande
Insomnia	Tall	–	Grande
Costa	Primo	Medio	Massimo
West Coast	Tall	–	Grande

Getting Around

South Dubliners love their **cars**, which goes some way towards explaining why traffic congestion is worse here than it is in Tokyo, London or Mexico City. The roads are particularly **clogged** early in the morning when, in addition to the regular commuter traffic, thousands of Southside mummies drive their **perfectly able-bodied**

children to school. Motorists will likely experience gridlock in the middle of the morning, too, when many Southside mummies go to meet 'the girls' for coffee, and again in the mid-afternoon, when they're out and about again to collect their pampered children from school. **Rush hour** begins shortly afterwards. If you are determined to drive in South Dublin, it's advised that you do so between midnight and 5 am, when there is usually a lull in the traffic flow.

An alternative is to use **public transport**, though visitors should be warned that the main suburban rail route, as well as most bus routes, pass through **working-class** areas, and you may find some of the images you'll see distressing, including **women in ski-pants sitting on walls, smoking**.

The Dart is a train service that follows the South Dublin coastline from Bray to Howth and carries tens of thousands of commuters from the suburbs into the City Centre every day. The route affords passengers some of the most breathtaking views to be had anywhere in Europe, including **Sandymount Strand** and the magnificent **Killiney Bay**. Bear in mind, however, that there are no first-class carriages on board and inquiries to **Iarnród Éireann** staff about the availability of toilet facilities may be met with a blunt, 'Where do you think you are – the **fooken Orient Express**?'

North of the Liffey there's rather less to look at as the

train traces a route through areas of Dickensian poverty, such as **Harmonstown** and **Kilbarrack**, where horses go up and down in the lifts of the local flats all day, just like in a **Roddy Doyle** film.

Those intrepid souls who are prepared to stay on for the entire hour-long journey, running the risk of being **robbed at knifepoint**, will notice the way the name of the service changes according to local dialects. In the well-off North Dublin suburbs of Howth, Sutton and Bayside, it's known as **'the Dort'**. As it passes through Kilbarrack, Killester and Harmonstown on its way to the City Centre, it becomes **'de Deert'**. When it crosses the Liffey, skirting the coast of Dublin 4, the vowel sound becomes softer again and it sounds more like **'the Doort'**. Through Glenageary, Dalkey and Killiney, it becomes **'the Doorsh'**. When it reaches Shankill, it's **'de fooken trayin'**, and by the time it reaches Bray, it's just **something people throw stones at**.

The **Luas** – or the Danny Day, as South Dubliners have lovingly christened it – is the jewel in the area's transport crown. The modern tram system is much like the generation it transports from the southern suburbs into the City Centre every morning – smooth, ambitious and liable to **crush anything that gets in its way**. It carries more than 100,000 passengers daily and operates at a profit, with no state subvention. It would be considered a model for public transport systems the world over if it didn't keep **crashing into cars and injuring people**.

There is also the option of a **Dublin bus** – though many South Dubliners will tell you they'd sooner climb aboard a **hijacked airbus**. With a new state-of-the-art fleet, bus users no longer run the risk of developing emphysema from diesel fumes, although the widespread, non-stop use of mobile phones among passengers does present a threat from **electromagnetic waves**. Scientists have estimated that spending fifteen minutes upstairs on a 46A at rush hour is the equivalent of sticking one's head in a 900-w microwave oven **for two days**.

Be aware, too, that you should try to have the exact amount ready to pay your bus fare. Due to robberies – mostly on **the Northside** – drivers no longer have access to a float. When you pay your fare, the money is entered into a chute and slides down into a safe hidden deep in the body of the bus. The safe is **time-locked, bullet-proof and encased in 6-ft of concrete**. Instead of change, you'll be given a **receipt** for the few cents you are owed, which is redeemable from Dublin Bus headquarters on O'Connell Street – a virtual **no-go area** for Southsiders.

If buses aren't your cup of tea, there is no end of **taxis** to ferry you about – at least between the hours of 2.00 and 4.00 in the afternoon. Be aware that almost all taxi drivers are from North Dublin and tend to think of themselves as **'characters'**. If you don't want to listen to unlikely stories involving stunning women paying their fares in sexual favours or their views on immigration, you should make this clear at the outset. Generally, when you state your destination, you'll be asked, 'What way do you want me to drive?' It's at that point you should say, 'Quietly.' Remember, **stories that could bring down governments** and **tirades against racial minorities** will be added to the surcharge.

Furthermore, many taxi drivers will take it upon themselves to bring you on a so-called **Phileas Fogg** –

A WORD FROM ROSS

If you're very brave – or more likely very hammered – you might try getting the Nightlink, a sort of public transport Paddy Wagon that brings drunks home in the early hours of the morning for whatever shrapnel they've left in their sky rockets after a night on the sauce. It wouldn't be unheard of for me to fall asleep on the old 'Fightlink' and be woken up in Donnybrook Bus Depot by some cleaner washing the jizz and vomit off the floor. Then, when you've regained your bearings, you've got to face the 'walk of shame' past all the drivers clocking on for the early shift.

around the world in eighty minutes. Try to consider this **low-level fraud** as part of the overall experience. Many visitors are in fact surprised by how little they're ripped off. It is customary to tip taxi drivers, rounding the fare up to the nearest €5 – or **whatever he demands** in return for letting you out of the car.

Theatre, Art and Literature

South Dublin boasts many outstanding works of art, a surprising number of which aren't in the hands of North Dublin's and West Dublin's **criminal gangs**.

The **National Gallery** houses a fine collection of quite stunning Western European art, including paintings by Caravaggio, Monet, Rubens, Gainsborough, Vermeer, Goya and Picasso, as well as Irish artists such as Jack B. Yeats. The gallery has had many **famous donors** down through the years, whose generosity ensured its doors remained open, including among their number **George Bernard Shaw**, **Sir Hugh Lane**, **Chester Beatty** and, in more recent times, rich middle-aged **ladies who lunch**, spending a fortune on cappuccinos and wedges of cake in the restaurant.

South Dubliners are regular visitors to the **Abbey**, **Peacock**, **Gate** and **Andrew's Lane** theatres and cause credit card booking lines to crash when Yungchen

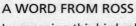

A WORD FROM ROSS

I was seeing this bird called Orna for a while, thick as bottled shite, roysh, but for some reason I wanted to impress her – probably because her old man was seriously loaded.

So one Saturday afternoon – it sounds focking mad now, even as I say it – I took her to the National Gallery to see the Turner Exhibition, this collection of supposedly impressive watercolours that they're only allowed to put on display in January because it's the best light, blahdy focking blah. Now, I've no interest in paintings whatsoever, but Orna's cracking on to be a real 'appreciator' of art. An hour we're in there, going from room to room.

So now we're, like, giving the Italian collection the once-over and Orna stops in front of Caravaggio's *The Taking of Christ*, stares at it with her hand up to her chin, then turns around to me – in front of the entire gallery – and at the top of her voice goes, 'How much is this one?'

I leaned in to her and tried to explain as gently and as quietly as I could that the paintings weren't for sale.

'Oh my God,' she said, 'why are we actually here then?'

Lhamo & Friends are doing whatever it is they do at the **National Concert Hall**. Remember to walk around the following day saying repeatedly, and in a raised voice, 'Oh, we caught the Overture to Egmont at the NCH last night. It's a triumph. I'll be SO mad at you if you don't catch it.'

As for books, South Dubliners tend to own **all the important ones**, some of which they intend reading one day.

Enough Dinner Party to Get By

During your stay in South Dublin, you might be fortunate enough to be invited to a dinner party. The talk here tends to centre around a small number of topics on which there is general agreement. Unless you are familiar with the consensus view, however, you can feel somewhat cut adrift from the rest of the company. Here are the main topics of conversation you'll hear discussed over dinner in a South Dublin home – and some safe opinions that are sure to impress.

The world

'It was absolute madness going into Iraq. Sure the CIA themselves said that it was ungovernable by democracy.

Now you're going to have civil war there. It was only ever about oil.'

'America always has to have a hate figure to fixate on. I mean, first Osama bin Laden was the new Hitler. Then it was Saddam Hussein. Now it's Kim Jong Il.'

'There's no actual link between global warming and climate change. I mean, it's suspected, but it's never actually been proven.'

'I actually like Michael Moore. It's just that you couldn't trust anything he says.'

'Now is *definitely* the time to go to Cuba because it's going to change overnight once Castro kicks the bucket.'

'I'm not actually in favour of a united Ireland. I mean, we've more in common with the English than we have with the people up there.'

'It's not famine that's responsible for Africa's problem. It's corruption.'

'Seventy per cent of Americans don't own a passport – and these people want to take over the world!'

'I'm not sure I buy the conspiracy theories, but there was definitely more to 9/11 than we'll ever find out.'

Politics

'Isn't Joe Higgins great, all the same? I'd never vote for him, but he's really good for politics.'

'Bertie Ahern's actually a hell of a lot cleverer than he lets on.'

'There's something about Michael McDowell I just don't trust.'

'When this country was in dire straits economically the Irish went to London, New York, pretty much everywhere, looking for work. They had to. Now people from countries less fortunate than ourselves want to come here. Let them, I say.'

'I'm actually all for immigration, but I do worry about whether there'll be a backlash when the recession comes. It happened in England.'

'The Chinese come here to work. The Romanians come here to beg. That's the difference.'

'You don't hear much about Travellers any more.'

'I agree with the idea of free education. But I also believe in giving my kids the best possible chance in life.'

'The Port Tunnel. E-Voting. The M50. We can't actually do anything right as a nation.'

Economics

'The property crash is coming, I'm telling you.'

'I hate Eddie Hobbs – but he talks a lot of sense.'

'The value of your home is absolutely meaningless unless you're going to sell it and live in a tent.'

'You would have had to have invested in the property market before 1995 to have made serious money from it.'

'Poland was the place to buy two years ago. We won't know where the place to buy now is for another two years. And by that time it'll be somewhere else.'

'They put up gas and electricity prices and blamed the price of oil. But then the price of oil came down and the bills stayed up. It's a disgrace.'

'I don't want to sound like a fuddy-duddy, but I have to say I miss the old Irish money.'

Shopping

'Tesco's actually do nicer food than Marks & Spencer now. They've basically out-Marks-&-Spencered Marks & Spencer.'

'I think Ikea can only be a good thing. It's going to breathe life back into the economy of . . . Ballymun, or wherever they're putting it.'

'The more time I spend in Dublin City Centre, the more it's starting to resemble the high street in every major city in the UK.'

'There's no good reason why organic vegetables should be twice the price of non-organic. That's why I just will not pay for them.'

'I admit I go to Aldi the odd time. Just for the cheap tinfoil, though. Me and half the crack addicts in Dublin.'

'We've actually just switched from PC to Mac. Did you know there're virtually no viruses available for Macs?'

Entertainment

'Okay, okay, this is going to sound really naff, but I actually enjoy Il Divo. We both do.'

'I have to say, even though I'm not from there, I have a real soft spot for the Munster rugby team.'

'I actually think Eddie O'Sullivan's brought the Irish team as far as he's going to bring them. Despite the three triple crowns.'

'Roy Keane at Sunderland? I mean, it's going to end in tears.'

'Colin Farrell's from an actual middle-class background. That accent's put on.'

'The funny thing about *Will & Grace* is that all of the gay characters in it are actually straight in real life.'

'I have to say I really enjoy Roisín Ingle's column in *The Irish Times* magazine – even though I'm a goy.'

'I actually can't see the point of reality TV. I mean, there're actually more interesting things happening in my sitting-room than there are in the *Big Brother* house.'

'Obviously I'm not a Westlife fan, but the thing about them is, they can all sing.'

Travel

'The M50 is a disgrace. It's like a car park. And the only obstruction that's causing the tailbacks is an artificial one – the toll booth.'

'Those speed traps are about raising revenue, nothing more. The problem is, if you know a speed limit is set too low, you're going to lose faith in all of the speed limits and end up ignoring them – even the sensible ones.'

'I'm not saying I'd ever drink and drive, but it's ridiculous that I'm considered a danger on the road after one pint and an eighty-five-year-old woman with failing eyesight isn't. I'm just saying . . . '

'It's obvious what's causing the mayhem on the roads. Ireland is the only country in the world where getting a driving licence is as easy as getting a TV licence.'

'Do NOT get me started on bus lanes. I'm *not* going there.'

'What about those tickets they give you on the bus instead of change? I've loads of them at home in a jar. I mean, you're never actually going to go back with them, are you?'

'All these people complaining about Ryanair – "It was only when I checked in that I remembered I had no legs, yet they refused point-blank to pick me up and carry me to the 'plane." As far as I'm concerned, you get what you pay for.'

Books

Occasionally the conversation will veer onto literature on its way back towards Eddie Hobbs. South Dubliners have opinions on many books they've never read. It's not important for you to have read them either. You just need a general idea of what they're about and an opinion that's likely to be met with general agreement. The following are the most talked about titles, together with a plausible comment that you can make about each one:

The Sea by John Banville

Synopsis: Art historian Max Morden returns to the seaside village where he spent his childhood summers to grieve for his deceased wife. Instead of finding repose, he is forced to confront another, forgotten trauma. A mesmerizing meditation on love and loss.

Do say: 'Banville's mastery of the English language is effortless and total. He was born out of his time. He deserves a Yeats, a Joyce or a Beckett for competition.

Instead he gets Dan Brown. That's his tragedy.'

Don't say: 'Who are Yeats, Joyce and Beckett?'

The Da Vinci Code by Dan Brown

Synopsis: When the curator of the Louvre museum is murdered, a sinister plot to silence the small circle of people guarding the true secret of the Holy Grail is revealed.

Do say: 'Absolute trash. Yeah, I read it – just to find out what all the fuss was about. It's actually very badly written. Have you read *Foucault's Pendulum* by Umberto Eco? Far superior.'

Don't say: 'Believe it or not, it's actually the only book I've ever finished.'

Any Harry Potter book by J.K. Rowling

Synopsis: The adventures of a young boy wizard.

Do say: 'I don't mind admitting that when a new one comes out, I end up fighting with the kids over who's going to read it first. I just think good and imaginative writing shouldn't be subjected to generational pigeon-holing.'

Don't say: 'I've seen the films – what's the point?'

The Curious Incident of the Dog in the Night-time by Mark Haddon

Synopsis: Christopher Boone is a fourteen-year-old boy with Asperger's Syndrome who sets out to investigate the killing of a neighbour's dog and finds his entire world turned upside-down.

Do say: 'Original and bitterly funny. Mark Haddon narrates the story of an autistic boy with a ventriloquist's skill and avoids lapsing into cliché, condescension or sentimentality.'

Don't say: 'Oh no, I focking hate weird kids. They freak me out.'

Freakonomics **by Steven D. Levitt and Stephen J. Dubner**

Synopsis: Levitt blows away our preconceptions about economics being a dull and unsexy branch of knowledge by using it to explore real world issues, like how drug gangs operate a similar corporate structure to McDonald's and how owning a gun is far less dangerous than owning a swimming pool.

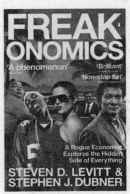

Do say: 'His linking of America's falling crime rate to its rising abortion rate shook the cosy consensus on the Left and the Right.'

Don't say: 'So is this dude, like, an American Eddie Hobbs?'

Never Let Me Go by Kazuo Ishiguro

Synopsis: Kathy, Ruth and Tommy grow up in a boarding school in the English countryside with the sense that they are somehow different from other kids. In later life, Kathy finally faces the truth about their seemingly idyllic childhood – and the future.

Do say: 'Moving and haunting. Forestalls all the uncomfortable questions about where science is taking us – and where we're taking science.'

Don't say: 'You only find out near the end that these

A WORD FROM FIONN

The major paradox as regards books is that, while more and more retail space is being given over to them, the range of choices for serious readers is actually narrowing all the time. The front-of-shop in all the major chain stores tends to be littered with women's fiction, diet books and the autobiographies of celebrities who aren't even a third of the way through their lives. That's the reason why pretty much everyone between the ages of eighteen and fifty is reading the same fifteen or twenty books, i.e. the titles I've listed above. I mean, is anyone reading Thomas Hardy, or Günter Grass, or Charles Dickens? Or Gustave Flaubert? Apart from me?

kids are clones who've been harvested for their organs. Oh, I hope that doesn't ruin it for you.'

Useful Facts

Water
The water in South Dublin is perfectly safe to drink. We'd recommend Volvic, Evian or Vittel.

Restrooms
Public restrooms on the Southside of Dublin are cleaner and safer than those on the Northside. When going to the toilet, different codes of etiquette apply on either side of the city. Among South Dublin males, for instance, the custom is to stand **outside the trough and urinate into it**, whereas in North Dublin the reverse is the case.

South Dublin is acknowledged as having some of the most spectacular restrooms – or, in the local parlance, **'jackses'**– in the world. The one on the top floor of **Brown Thomas** on Grafton Street could have been taken, lock, stock and golden taps, from the home of Montgomery Burns. Gentle classical music – perhaps Beethoven's 'Moonlight Sonata' or even Mozart's 'Elvira Madigan Piano Concerto' – is piped into the room, sending you into a state of Zen-like calm as you **drain the lizard** (number ones) or **drop the kids off at the**

pool (number twos). Once the heavy work is done, you'll make your way to the sink area, where a very nice attendant will twist one of the gold taps for you and give you a couple of squirts of pleasant-smelling **Molton Brown** fine liquid handwash (*nettoyant pour les mains*). A clean, white towel made of the **finest Egyptian cotton** will then be proffered to allow you to dry your Christian Andersens, after which you'll have the option of moisturising, using some soothing Molton Brown hand lotion. Similar restrooms in the **Conrad**, **Westbury**, **Merrion** and **Westin** hotels ensure that

THE SIGNS FOR MALE AND FEMALE TOILETS IN SOUTH DUBLIN:

Male   Female

taking a Donald Trump on the Southside is a purely pleasurable experience.

Imitation is, of course, the sincerest form of flattery, and several establishments on the Northside have attempted to provide a low-rent version of the same service. A common feature of many nightclub toilets is the **non-national, minimum-wage flunky** who charges up to €1 for a couple of blasts of deodorant, which is still considered a luxury in North Dublin. At hourly intervals he will also use a thick-bristled brush to sweep the urine into the trench to make the floor look less like a **giant foot-spa**.

Medical Emergencies

A large number of hospitals and clinics on the Southside perform essential **cosmetic surgery**. In 2006, 1.2 million procedures were carried out in South Dublin – that's more than California and Florida combined. In fact, augmentation – better known as 'aug' – is the number one most requested birthday and Christmas present among females between the ages of eighteen and twenty-four.

South Dublin people are regarded as among **the most beautiful in the world**, which puts pressure on young girls, in particular, to have defects in form and function corrected by surgery. Mammaplasties, or **breast enlargements**, are now performed more often than dental fillings, and it's estimated that the amount

of silicone used to enhance South Dublin 'boobs' in an average year would be sufficient to tyre a fleet of **50,000 cars** – and put a spare in every boot.

Each year an estimated 60,000 South Dublin women undergo a rhytidectomy, or **'face-lift'**, often as a gift to mark a significant **wedding anniversary** or the onset of the **menopause**. It's not uncommon for friends of twenty, thirty or even forty years not to recognize each other after such procedures, and you will sometimes hear wealthy, middle-aged women asking one another, 'But how do I know it's definitely you?'

A rhinoplasty is an operation to **reshape the nose** to make it look less like a rhinoceros horn and it is fast growing in popularity. So too are otoplasties (**reshaping the ear**), abdominoplasties (**tummy tucks**), **chin augmentations** and **suction-assisted lipectomies**, which involve the removal of fat from the bodies of people who just can't stop feeding their faces by inserting the hose of a hoover up the patient's **jaxy**. Much of this waste matter is preserved in large vats and subsequently reused in **buttock augmentation**, which involves the grafting of fat onto the buttocks to give them a more **pert** definition and make them look less like **two Transits fighting over a parking space**.

Most dentists in South Dublin will perform **teeth whitenings** – the application of hydrogen peroxide to the teeth to bleach them – at short notice, or no notice at all.

For all other medical emergencies, dial **999**.

Vaccinations

South Dublin is **free of all major diseases**. However, those visitors who are planning trips further afield to North or West Dublin or to rural areas (see pages 313–18) would be well advised to get vaccinated against cholera, diphtheria, typhoid, yellow fever, rabies, polio, hepatitis A, B and C, tetanus, mastitis, ringworm and liver fluke.

Driving

It is not necessary to pass a **driving test** to take a car out onto the roads of South Dublin. Most locals don't bother to apply for a full driving licence because the waiting list to sit the test is now years long. Instead, they drive under a **provisional licence**. Getting your hands on one of these is about as difficult as **having a birthday**. Provisional licences are issued subject to certain requirements and restrictions, and it's not unheard of for **overly officious** members of the Garda Síochána to pull over provisional licence-holders and demand to know why they're driving on motorways, driving without a qualified driver in the car or driving without L-plates displayed. The custom for **young women** in such situations is to say, 'Oh my God,' over and over again, along with the occasional 'I cannot believe you are *actually* giving me a hord time about this,' and 'You have SUCH an attitude problem,' before eventually resorting to tears. **Young men** generally issue veiled threats, such as, 'Do you know who my old man is?' or the more pointed, 'You are SO getting your orse sued.'

Remember: these driving regulations are seldom enforced and, even when they are, result in a fine of no more than **a few thousand euro**.

There are a number of variations to the standard rules of the road as they apply in South Dublin. On dual-carriageways and motorways, the left lane is for those driving **within the speed limit**, while the right is for those who wish to drive **in excess of the speed limit**. The exception to this rule is women drivers, who are permitted to drive in either lane at any speed they like. Similarly, the approach to **roundabouts** is different for women than it is for men. When intending to take the first exit off a roundabout, a **man** will indicate left on the approach. If the intention is to take the second exit, he will not indicate at all on the approach to the roundabout until he has passed the first exit; then he will indicate left. If he intends to take any subsequent exit, he will indicate right on his approach to the roundabout and then, just before he reaches the correct exit, signal left. **Women** generally won't signal at all – except perhaps with their middle finger should someone sound their car horn to express annoyance at their **lack of basic courtesy**.

When waiting to enter a main road from a T-junction, it is customary for male drivers already on the main road to **suddenly accelerate** to prevent you from pulling out in front of them; or, if you have already completed the manoeuvre, to speed up and then brake hard, stopping just inches away from your rear bumper, to give you the impression that you have **almost caused an accident**. They do something similar on roundabouts, too.

On the plus side, if any motorist slows down to allow you to pull out from, for instance, a car park or side street, it will almost certainly be a male driver. It is virtually unheard of for women in South Dublin to show such civility, and many would sooner pull into a **yellow box** than allow another car to join the flow of traffic in front of them.

At the same time, South Dublin women not only expect men to be chivalrous on the road, they consider it an inalienable right. If you slow down to allow a woman to change lanes in front of you, or stop to allow one to cross a lane of traffic travelling in the opposite direction, don't expect a **wave of acknowledgement** or any gesture that conveys gratitude. You will only be disappointed. A look of **frosty unconcern** or **sulky petulance** is more the norm. Consider anything other than that a pleasant bonus.

A WORD FROM OISINN

Working, as I do, in the cosmetics industry, it'd be fair to say that I know women. And take it from me, they're all Baghdad especially when Munster are playing at home! Bear this in mind when attempting to overtake one on a single-lane stretch of road. Birds are quite happy to drive at 40-km per hour on a road where the speed limit is twice that, but the very moment you cross the median with the intention of overtaking one, she'll immediately consider this an affront to her pride and will floor the accelerator, leaving you with the choice of either getting behind her again or enjoying a head-on collision with a car coming in the opposite direction. That's birds for you!

And now please turn the page and note some essential South Dublin road signs – they will save you from all manner of catastrophes . . .

DANGER: SLOW DRIVERS
IN AREA

PUB AHEAD

ONE-CAR FAMILY AREA

OLD DEARS AHEAD

WORKING-CLASS AREA.
LOCK WINDOWS

VERY WORKING-CLASS AREA.
TURN BACK

CONSTRUCTION WORKERS
AHEAD. WOLF-WHISTLING AND
OBSCENE HAND GESTURES
LIKELY

CAUTION: WOMEN
DRIVERS THINKING ABOUT
SHOES AHEAD

RELAX! MIDDLE-CLASS
AREA AHEAD

ROUNDABOUT AHEAD.
STOP TEXTING

COUNTRYSIDE AHEAD.
SHUT WINDOWS

ARGUMENTS WITH FELLOW
MOTORISTS LIKELY. DO NOT
BACK DOWN

Cars

An **SUV** is the ideal vehicle for tackling the hard, desert terrain of the Sahara, gripping treacherous, hoarfrost-covered Alpine roads – or dropping your children to their South Dublin fee-paying school. Sports Utility Vehicles have received a lot of bad press in recent years, mainly because driving one for an hour is the equivalent, in fuel-consumption terms, of leaving all the lights on in your house for 1,000 years, **or something**. There are now 212,000 SUVs in South Dublin – that's one per household. The energy required to power that lot for a day is equivalent to that given off by **the sun** in a week.

In fairness to the usually eco-friendly **Southside mummies** who drive SUVs, many of South Dublin's most prestigious schools are located in mountainous areas that are impossible to negotiate in an ordinary car. **Mount Anville**, for instance, is 15,000 ft above sea level, and its approach roads are covered in snow most of the year, while **Blackrock College** is located at the top of a slope pitched like the north face of the Eiger.

Southside daddies are partial to German-made cars that are built like Panzer tanks, reflecting their own *Blitzkrieg* approach to life. They tend to drive **BMWs**, **Mercedes** and other cars that are not so much vehicles as **living rooms on wheels**. They also like their cars to have as many gadgets as possible, to help them pass the **three hours** they spend each day commuting the short distance to and from their place of work.

Satellite navigation – or 'Sat Nav' – is enormously popular, especially when **driving home pissed** from the golf club on a Saturday evening. Most 'big cars' now come with a computer-style mouse, which operates everything from the air conditioning – a must, given South Dublin's boiling summer temperatures – to the volume on the Dire Straits' *Brothers In Arms* CD that comes as standard.

On the road, South Dublin daddies always want to overtake you, regardless of what speed you're doing. They tend to appear suddenly in your rear-view mirror, riding on your back bumper, flashing their hazard lights at you as a warning to pull into the hard shoulder and let them pass. Once they've completed the manoeuvre, they proceed at **exactly the same speed you were driving at in the first place**.

For **Southside boys**, the **Golf GTI** is still the coolest thing on four wheels. As far as cars go, they're old school, yes, but you can't argue with the fact that they **go like UCD freshers** and that girls are seriously impressed by them. Once they start earning their own money and stop living off their parents, South Dublin boys are inclined towards **BMWs** with soft tops, ideal for cruising under South Dublin's hot sun.

South Dublin girls generally start off driving their mothers' **Fiat Puntos** or **Volkswagen Polos**, then graduate onto something with **character**, such as **Volkswagen Beetles**, **Mini Coopers** or **Mini Convertibles**, in baby-pink, naturally. A huge number of these are bought by fathers as eighteenth or twenty-first birthday presents for their daughters, and no greater love can a man have for his little princess than to offer it with an occasion-specific number plate, such as **07 D 18 or 07 D 21**.

The **Volkswagen Eos** is also an enormously popular choice. It was named after the Greek Goddess of the Dawn, who, according to legend, had a curse placed upon her that turned her into a **nymphomaniac** – making her the ideal role model for thousands of South Dublin girls. It's a compact little car, but can quite comfortably accommodate five girls **with eating disorders**.

South Dublin on a Shoestring: Getting by on Ten Grand a Day

South Dublin is now more expensive than Paris – or even Tokyo. But even for visitors operating on a tight budget, there is still plenty to do. Here are three suggested itineraries that will set you back less than **€10,000 per day**.

Day 1

Spend an excellent night in the new, Aidan Cavey-
designed Penthouse at the Merrion Hotel (€2,450),
enjoying a five-star breakfast and a soak in the
cedarwood hot-tub on the rooftop terrace to prepare
you for a day of culture. Visit the Apollo Gallery on
Duke Street to browse through hundreds of works
by contemporary Irish artists. Buy a Graham Knuttel
original (€5,000). Go back to bed (€2,450).
Total cost: €9,900

Day 2

Wake up in the sumptuous surrounds of the Conrad
Hotel's Presidential Suite (€1,200), and enjoy a leisurely
breakfast in front of the lounge's giant plasma-screen
television to steel yourself for a day of heavy-duty
shopping. 'Do' Grafton Street. Visit the Decent Cigar
Emporium and pick up a box of ten Cuban Davidoffs
(€1,500), then buy a Cartier watch from Weir & Sons
(€1,700). Surprise the woman in your life with a
genuine ermine coat (€2,500) from Barnardo. Enjoy
lunch and a bottle of excellent wine at La Stampa
(€300), before taking a taxi (€50, including tip) to
Cavistons fine food emporium in Sandycove. Pick up
a few ounces of Beluga caviar (€300) and return to
Grafton Street (€50, including tip) to enjoy afternoon
tea for two (€100, including tip) at the Westbury Hotel.
Enjoy steak and chips with onion rings and another

bottle of excellent wine (€840) at Shanahan's on the Green. Take a taxi back to the Conrad Hotel (€30, including unnecessary detour) for another night in the Presidential Suite (€1,200).

Total cost: €9,770

Day 3

Enjoy a night of opulence in the Presidential Suite of the Four Seasons Hotel in Ballsbridge (€2,520), taking breakfast on the terrace while enjoying the city's roofscape. Hire a helicopter (€1,200 per flying hour) to chopper you and a friend to the K Club in County Kildare. Enjoy a round of golf on the famous Palmer course (€370 each). Toast your victory with a lunch of Dublin Bay prawns, roast rack of lamb with minted couscous and a bottle of Champagne (€250, plus €50 tip) in the Legends Restaurant overlooking the 18th green, before choppering back to Dublin (€1,200) and relaxing for an hour or two in the Ice Bar at the Four Seasons. Enjoy five or six Champagne Mojitos each (€228, plus €30 tip) before taking a taxi into Dublin City Centre (€50, including tip) for dinner and a bottle of extremely good wine at the plush Restaurant Patrick Guilbaud at the Merrion Hotel (€950, plus €50 tip). Return to the Four Seasons for a second night in the Presidential Suite (€2,520).

Total cost: €9,788

The South Dublin wake-up call.

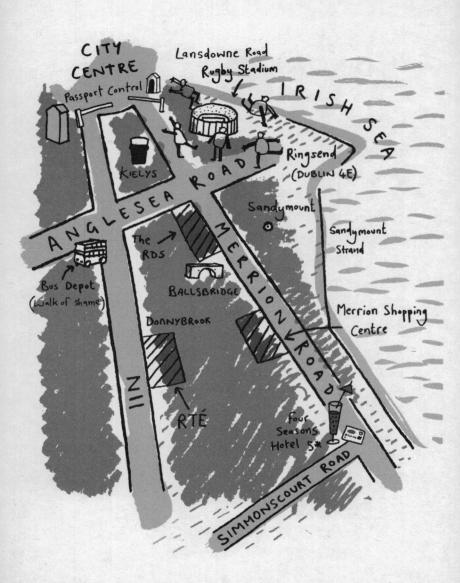

1. Dublin 4

Neighbourhoods don't come any better than this! D4 – as its understandably smug residents call it – is Ireland's most prestigious postal district, home to South Dublin's true blue-bloods and the setting for some of the most expensive real estate in Europe.

It's a place of untold wealth – untold because most of it is offshore, out of sight of the Revenue Commissioners and the various tribunals of investigation that have tried to ram a stake into the heart of this area. It's safe to say, though, that Dublin 4 has more billionaires per square mile than anywhere else in Ireland . . .

The area, which starts south of the Grand Canal, is made up of four affluent districts – Ballsbridge, Donnybrook, Sandymount and Mount Merrion – and two poor ones – Ringsend and Irishtown – which most well-heeled locals would like to see redesignated Dublin 4E, or even **reclaimed by the sea**.

Ballsbridge is D4's **command centre**, named after Knightsbridge, the fashionable district in London's West End on which it has modelled itself. Most of the vital points on South Dublin's compass are here: Lansdowne Road, the RDS, the Berkeley Court, the Dublin Horse Show, the Four Seasons and the headquarters of AIB. Also here are the two most expensive streets on the Monopoly board, **Ailesbury Road** and **Shrewsbury Road**, home to South Dublin's old money business and professional classes and a large number of embassies

and diplomatic residences. At the centre of it all is Herbert Park, Dublin 4's one remaining green lung, which oxygenates the downtown idyll that is Ballsbridge.

Donnybrook's most famous contribution to the world is its name, which is a synonym for a scene of uproar or violent disorder. The term originates from an ancient fair that was held in the town and was notorious for its scenes of **drunkenness**. It was banned in 1855, and Donnybrook hasn't looked back since. (Although the scenes of drunkenness are a tradition it has retained, particularly around the time of rugby matches.) Now a wealthy suburb, Donnybrook is home to the Leinster rugby team, the world-famous Kielys pub and the CIÉ bus depot, where waking up still pissed after missing your stop is a rite of passage in the lives of most D4 teenagers.

Sandymount (/sen-d-mine-t/) is a well-to-do seaside town, at the heart of which is an English-style **village green**, encircled by fashionable shops, restaurants and art galleries.

Mount Merrion (/mine-t-merrion/), while also ridiculously posh, exists mainly to provide a **buffer zone** between Dublin 4 and the salubrious, but far less affluent, Booterstown.

Many of Ireland's most elite schools – Mount Anville, Alexandra College, St Conleth's, St Michael's College and Gonzaga – are in Dublin 4, or are no more than a

On summer's evenings, the stressed-out denizens of Dublin 4 can at least retire to Sandymount's golden strand to pick coconuts and play beach volleyball with Playboy bunnies.

Callaway drive away. The area has maintained its exclusivity by remaining well **outside the price range** of the Celtic Tiger's *arriviste* generation. New money won't buy you an ivy-coloured Georgian pile in the embassy belt, a Victorian red-brick terraced house in leafy Sandymount or a mini palazzo on one of those blue-chip Monopoly streets – only **mad money** will. Property prices here are impervious to market trends. Houses change hands for whatever the billionaire buyer is willing to pay. In 2006 Denis O'Brien paid **€35**

million for a seven-bedroom house on two thirds of an acre on Shrewsbury Road. His stamp duty alone would have bought an entire cul de sac in many parts of this divided city. In 2005 the house opposite O'Brien's was sold for a record **€58 million**. One of O'Brien's new neighbours, the property developer Sean Dunne, has been buying up landmark sites in Ballsbridge – including Jurys Hotel – and in 2006 bought land from AIB at a cost of **€55 million per acre**.

The people who are simply *stinking* rich, as opposed to *noxiously* rich, have been forced out to Ranelagh, Clonskeagh and other parts of Dublin 6, which is trying to style itself as a kind of **Dublin 4W**, but with no success. The simple truth is: nowhere else in Ireland is like D4. Where else but this part of town could have **four cricket clubs** – and only one GAA club?

The people you'll find at the end of D4's pebbled driveways know how to live – it's all corporate boxes, garden parties and endless days of golf with Dermot Desmond, John Magnier and JP McManus. A visit to this privileged corner of the world is an unforgettable experience. But do it soon. Economists predict that by 2056 it will be **too expensive** for even the wealthiest people in the world to live here – and it will become a desolate waste land.

History of Dublin 4

It would be true to say that Dublin 4 has existed for as long as Northsiders have smelt bad. It was founded some time around the seventh century as a **sanctuary** from Dublin's peasantry, who had turned the once respectable area north of the River Liffey into a lawless war zone. A few hundred people who wanted to live in peace and prosperity gathered up their **meagre possessions** – wine coolers, fondu sets, cappuccino frothers – and crossed the river, like the ancient Israelites fleeing Egypt, for a new life in a place where they suspected property prices would soon go through the roof. They called this beautiful land – close to the sea and within easy walking distance of fashionable Grafton Street – Dublin For The Wealthy, which was eventually shortened to Dublin For, then finally became Dublin Four, or D4.

Famous Residents

Sandymount has been home to two of Ireland's most well-known hellraisers – **W B Yeats** and **Colin Farrell**. Nobel Prize-winner **Seamus Heaney** also lives here, while former Taoiseach **Albert Reynolds** and former

Tánaiste **Mary Harney** both live in D4. In separate houses, obviously.

Stating the names of one's neighbours in D4 is a legal minefield. This smart corner of town is home to tens of thousands of people with **tax exile** status, who are allowed to spend no more than 183 days in Ireland each year. It's virtually impossible to state that anyone else lives in Dublin 4 without libelling them.

Shopping

Dublin 4 women are famed the world over for their lack of embarrassment. Just about the only thing that'll cause them discomfiture is turning up at a social event in the same outfit as somebody else – especially if the photographs are going to appear in *Image* magazine. This trait explains the proliferation of boutiques where women can buy something classic that isn't sharing a rack with forty other items of the same style in Coast or Oasis. Shops like **Havana** and **Marian Gale** in Donnybrook, **Compagnie L** in the Merrion Shopping Centre and **Aura** in Sandymount have been dressing posh ladies for donkeys' years, whether it's evening dress, a frock for young Tiernan and Sophie's wedding or a trouser suit in ivory for that charity fundraiser.

Massive televisions are all the rage in South Dublin, and they don't come any more massive – or expensive –

than at **Bang & Olufsen** in Donnybrook. Power City this ain't! You can be assured there are no 'Bush 32-inch televisions – only €99.99' or 'jug kettles – only €9.99' in this joint. This is the home of the €4,000 CD player and the €20,000 television, although calling it 'a television' is like saying that Brian O'Driscoll plays the odd bit of rugby. These are plasma screen, HD-ready, home-cinema units, and there are people in this part of the world who sit and watch them for hours – without ever turning them on.

Most busy D4 couples have time for just the one token child. During the latter stages of pregnancy, many mums- and dads-to-be head for **Limari**, a wonderful children's furniture shop in Donnybrook, to start preparing the royal bedroom for the arrival of The Chosen One. There, you can buy a custom-made cot with your child's name on it (hyphenated names are extra – they charge by the barrel) or a bed designed in the manner of a yacht – just the style for the kid who will one day take the wheel of the family Lürssen.

In the Merrion Shopping Centre there is a shop that might well qualify as The Most South Dublin Shop In The Entire World. **Amélie**, an excellent shop with friendly staff, sells golf- and skiwear for ladies, which means pink plus-fours, snazzy sun visors in baby-blue, golf balls in your signature colour . . . Have you ever heard of a shop more appropriately positioned?

Tinned sardines were once considered the food of

the peasantry, but now they're the height of chic. Dublin 4 has taken those big, fat, Brittany-bred *sardines millésimées* to its heart, and, even at €8 a tin, gourmet shops just can't stack their shelves quickly enough. **Terroirs**, the superb wine shop in Donnybrook, has started importing the famous Maison Albert Ménès brand that all of D4 is having on its toast on a Saturday morning.

   Ballsbridge Motors is where the locals go to celebrate their commission on that bonds deal or their astronomical fee from their work at that tribunal by buying a soft-top tank. How about the SL 350 in obsidian-black metallic with pebble-beige leather interior – only €136,000?

A WORD FROM ROSS

The RDS is where they have what we used to call the Ancient Geek Olympics, in other words the Young Scientist of the Year competition. Probably comes as a surprise to no one, roysh, that Fionn is a previous winner. He – and I'm reading this from an article about him in *The Irish Times* that I have pinned to a dort board – discovered a new compound similar to zinc that almost merited inclusion in the periodic table of elements. You can't say that's focking roysh! The goy was, like, fourteen. He should have been out, chorming the birds, trying to get his first bit of knocker, instead of whacking off to his science book in his room.

I remember the day of the exhibition, roysh, because that was one scary day. The old man had been asking me for weeks what I was – get this – 'putting forward' for the exhibition, like I couldn't decide between the space rocket I made out of washing-machine ports that could orbit the Earth and the cure I'd invented for cancer. He used to mistake me for some kind of misunderstood genius, see. When he asked me that, I just blanked him – what with him being a total penis and everything – and he took it to mean that I was playing my cards close to my chest. He went, 'Aaa-ha!' and tapped the side of his nose. So I tapped him for two hundred sheets – materials, I told the stupid focker. Then I hit Ballsbridge.

You should have actually seen the RDS that day? The Nerd Herd was there in force. This one goy – a kipper from Michael's – was driving around in a solar-powered cor, and I'm not yanking your chain here. Another had discovered a new vaccine for malaria that had no side-effects. I'd be shocked if any of these geeks know what a bird looks like naked – even today.

Of course, I felt as thick as shite wandering around looking at all this stuff, so I decided, roysh, to basically steal somebody else's work and pass it off as my own. So I stole – you guessed it – the solar-powered cor. Stole is probably the wrong word. I suppose you could say I actually corjacked the little peach-fuzz focker who made it, hit him a few slaps around the head and threw him out onto the ground.

So I'm pegging it around the Simmonscourt Pavilion on this little thing, wondering where the focking judges are, when all of a sudden these two security gords step out in front of me – the little focker had sung like a box of crickets, as Ronan would say. I took a shorp left to avoid them, clattering into – and basically making shit of – this bird's investigation into the effects of geography on elite athletic performance. All you could hear was the crash of glass and all this, like, screaming and of course the next thing I knew I was being dumped on my orse on Simmonscourt Road.

I got four phone numbers, though – two Mounties, one Loreto Foxrock and one Muckross, while Fionn was still a virgin at twenty. So you tell me, who was the real winner that day?

How to Get Around

Dublin 4 is regarded by many as not so much a geographic location with set boundaries as a transcendent state of being. Happily, this liberation from the effects of karma and bodily existence *is* serviced by both bus and rail. There are Dart stations at **Lansdowne Road** and **Sandymount** (both about less than ten minutes' walk from Ballsbridge and Sandymount villages), and one at **Sydney Parade** (which is a five-minute walk from Merrion).

As for buses, well, they throw those numbers at you like a bingo-caller on speed.

Sandymount has the **2, 3, 5, 7, 7A** and **18**. Ballsbridge is serviced by the **5, 7, 7A, 7N, 8, 18, 27X** and **45**. You'll get to Donnybrook on the **7B, 7D, 10, 10A, 18, 32X, 41X, 46A, 46B, 46C, 46D, 46E, 46N, 46X, 58C, 58X, 84X, 145, 746**, the **Vengabus**, the **Magic Bus** and probably even the ***bualadh bos***.

Where to Stay 🏛

Accommodation key:
Luxury ★★★
Seriously opulent ★★★★
Pretty much palatial ★★★★★

★★★ The Herbert Park Hotel, Ballsbridge

The Herbert 'Pork' is a seriously la-di-dah hotel in the heart of D4's financial district, described, in true estate agent-speak, as being 'enclosed by **an Eden of leafy trees**'. Everything is designed for your comfort and convenience – **king-size beds** and **PlayStations** in every room, and a restaurant with a sun terrace that overlooks the famous Herbert Park. Despite the Eden reference and the hotel's close proximity to the canal, don't come wandering in here at 4.00am with a hooker. Hotels this swanky don't do rooms on a meter rate.

★★★★ The Berkeley Court Hotel, Ballsbridge

'The Barkley' is more than just a famous landmark in this old Georgian neighbourhood, it's also the heart that beats life into Dublin 4. This smart, five-star hotel, where Frank Sinatra once stayed, is as much a **social institution** as the Savoy is in London or the Ritz is in Paris, where socialites and professionals, sportsmen and stars of the silver screen come to relax and shoot the breeze over fine whiskeys or rare brandies. The hotel describes its service as reflecting 'the charm and manners of times past', which means that from the time you step into the big, opulent, chandelier-lit lobby, everyone talks to you like you're their **lord and master**, which is just how they like it around here. Get there early on the day of an international match at Lansdowne Road and listen to some of D4's finest *bon vivants* discussing rugby at an **annoyingly boisterous** decibel level.

★★★★★ The Four Seasons, Ballsbridge

'Location of cosmopolitan experience, blah blah blah, handsome architectural design, waffle waffle waffle, atmosphere of traditional comfort and ease, blahdy blahdy blah' . . . no adjective-happy copywriter could do justice to this little piece of **heaven**. This is a hotel so upmarket they practically give you a title with your room key. A suite here will cost you almost 600 bills a night, but for that they'll unpack and iron your clothes, clean your room not once but twice a day and **shine your shoes** while you watch the CNN business report in your complimentary terry bathrobe. There's a two-line telephone in your room and a **limo** waiting outside the door, ready to take you wherever you want to go, which, believe us, won't be far because downstairs you have the Ice Bar and Four Seasons restaurant.

You'll never want to leave. Visa or Mastercard might eventually recommend it, though.

Wesley Disco

Wesley Disco is an institution in South Dublin. Without it, literally thousands of fifteen- and sixteen-year-olds would still be virgins today. A night out involving 'Wes' is the alcohol-fuelled precursor to many young teenagers **'doing it'** for the first time, and the famous pre-mating rituals involved could occupy an anthropologist for a lifetime.

The famous Wesley Disco has kept alive the time-honoured South Dublin tradition of teenage girls dressing up as hookers, drinking copious amounts of vodka, getting off with a best friend's boyfriend, being sick in the car bringing them home and then spending the rest of their teenage years claiming that – oh my God – their drink must *have been spiked that night.*

It starts early in the evening, when hundreds of moms and dads arrive in a fleet of Volvos and Tourans and deposit their children outside **Eddie Rocket's** or **Abrakebabra**. The girls, sensibly dressed in jeans, boots and rolled-neck sweaters, occupy and secure every public convenience in the area to strip down into their **real outfit** for the night, which could best be described as not so much a strapless evening dress as a dressless evening strap. Once their parents disappear, Morehampton Road suddenly resembles a streetwalkers' convention, as barely pubescent but heavily made-up girls in **micro-minis** and **six-inch pencil heels** totter around with their **Crouching Tiger** (Hidden Naggin) concealed about their person.

The traffic grinds to a standstill as taxi drivers slow down to rubberneck and make inappropriately lewd comments to embarrassed passengers. The whole of Donnybrook chokes in a miasma of Issey Miyake as the young adolescents, having knocked back half their vodka, disappear into the disco.

When it comes to getting off with boys, the girls set each other **targets** for the evening. The bar is usually set at five, but the gold standard is said to be twenty-five. These young people then 'get to know each other' with tongues and full-body contact. Coupling usually takes place in a field or laneway or, if you're really lucky, on the sofa in a mate's gaff. The girls go home the following morning, having 'stayed at a friend's'.

A WORD FROM JP

I don't want to come across as some kind of fuddy-duddy who's old before his time – and I know it's not realistic in this day and age to expect people to keep their virginity until the day they marry – but I find the level of licentiousness among young people quite disturbing. Young girls, in particular, seem to have no respect for their bodies, which are, after all, tabernacles for the Holy Spirit and only ours on loan. I can't say this without feeling like something of a hypocrite, for when I was sixteen I, too, sowed my oats indiscriminately. And yes, it satisfied me in that instant, but it left me feeling spiritually bereft. That's what led me to the Lord.

I'm not one to go waving the Old Testament in people's faces, but there's a story in the Book of Genesis about two towns you may have heard of – we're talking Sodom and Gomorrah – which were wiped off the face of the Earth by God because of the wickedness of their inhabitants. A couple of years ago I was lucky enough to visit the Holy Land, and I went to the point at the southern end of the Dead Sea where those two towns once stood. It's true that no ruins have ever been recovered, but there are strange salt formations on the seabed that suggest they really did exist. Bitumen deposits have also been uncovered, which are mentioned in the description of the destruction of the towns in Genesis 14:10.

A guy I met out there, who was a geologist, told me that an earthquake – caused by God, obviously – probably brought about a mass inferno that melted the bitumen and sucked Sodom and Gomorrah into the Earth. Now, I'm not comparing them to Donnybrook and Ballsbridge, but I think there is a lesson in there for all of us.

Where to Eat

Roly's Bistro in Ballsbridge might well be the most popular restaurant in Dublin – even if it is a bit too friendly and inexpensive for some Southside palates. Whether you're there for lunch, the early bird or evening *à la carte*, there's always a bustle about the place, and people come as much for the buzz as for the superb classical French cooking with a nod – more like a high-five – to honest-to-goodness Irish traditions. The atmosphere will be right up your street, especially if your street happens to be Shrewsbury Road, while the food – spiced Castletownbere crab *won tons* with avocado salad, or traditional Kerry lamb and vegetable pie – is simply wondrous. As they say in Dublin 4, you can't kid a Bistro Kid.

Set in a red-brick terraced house, **The Lobster Pot** in Ballsbridge is one of Dublin dining's best-kept secrets. Its regulars sometimes finish a meal by toasting the continued success of Roly's next door, as it means this 25-year-old, family-run restaurant remains their exclusive preserve. The service is smart, the fish and shellfish out of this world – check out the Lobster Newburg – and the décor is stylishly olde worlde, all polished brass and tapestries, bathed in the glow from a big open fire that roars like . . . well, like a big red crustacean in a pot of boiling water.

Louis Walsh has become **The Four Seasons'** equivalent of Fawlty Towers' resident, Major.

ROLY'S BREAD

Roly's Bistro's baked-to-order bread is famous in these parts, and now you can buy it 'to go'. On Sunday evenings you'll see hundreds of women queueing around the block for a loaf, like they once did in Jaruzelski's Poland – except it'd be more spinach and raisin, or rye and linseed, these women would be after, for their children's school lunches, obviously.

Fortunately, that hasn't stopped the hotel restaurant becoming one of South Dublin's favourites, which is down to the great food and the bang-on service. D4 types like to be waited on, but not fussed over. Here, the waiting staff have a preternatural ability to anticipate your every whim, see to it before you have to ask and disappear again as quickly as they materialized. Half of the residents on Ailesbury Road haven't used their Agas since this joint opened.

As the name suggests, **Itsa 4** is for people who know where they're from and aren't shy about advertising the fact. The down-to-earth food and the ergonomically designed baby chairs have made it a favourite lunch place for yummy-mummies meeting Judie Dench-type glammy grannies.

The jewel in the Sandymount crown is **Dunne & Crescenzi**, however, an Italian restaurant much revered by media types for its authentic Italian staff and excellent but inexpensive trattoria fare. If they tripled their prices, this could become D4's favourite eatery. They won't, of course.

The people of Dublin 4 are a special breed, and they won't eat any old muck – unless, of course, it's organic and fabulously expensive. The area has a number of excellent gourmet food shops, including **Michael Byrne Fine Foods** in Sandymount and the **Douglas Food Company** in Donnybrook.

Eddie Rocket's is a chain of 1950s-style American

diners that serve hamburgers, onion rings and enormous shakes to rich kids, against a soundtrack of Elvis Presley, Buddy Holly and Bobby Darin hits. The American accents affected by most of the customers contribute to the sense of being trapped on the set of *Happy Days*. Going to Ed's, as it's known, is a rite of passage for many South Dublin teens, and the restaurant in Donnybrook is probably the most famous outlet in this respect. Their first visit there will invariably be on a Saturday afternoon with friends, while their moms or dads wait outside in the Lexus, engrossed in *The Irish Times* magazine or *Golf World*. Within a year or two their little charges will be going by themselves, lining their stomachs with cheese and bacon fries, then changing out of their school uniforms in the toilets, before trying to pass themselves off as eighteen in the local pubs.

Donnybrook Fair 🍦

Donnybrook Fair is *the* mothership of fine food emporiums and proof that the people of Dublin 4 will buy anything as long as it's made by a small cottage industry in Connemara and costs a tenner a jar. The customers of this smart little mini-mart want their shopping baskets to reflect their **smug** sense of themselves. They don't want bread; they want onion and bacon loaf. They don't want custard creams; they want cantucci biscuits. They don't want virgin olive oil; they want *virgine* olive oil, which is the same as the other stuff but costs €11 per bottle. Yes, this is where Dublin 4 stocks its double-door Smegs with **quail eggs**, **Dutch-smoked Gouda** and **organic sheep's milk**.

The clientele you'll encounter here are moms and dads with far too much money; gay men, who are known affectionately as the Donnybrook Fair-ies; and sulky, stick-thin women in their twenties who **dress to kill** just to nip out to the shop to buy melba toast – their sole source of nourishment.

An hour spent perusing the shelves in here is an insight into how 'the other half' lives. You'll step out onto Morehampton Road, clutching your American-style paper grocery bag with its distinctive D/F logo, with your pockets considerably lightened – but your spirits lightened, too.

Pubs and Clubs

Kielys of Donnybrook is by far the most famous pub on this side of the city, and it's as South Dublin as high-fiving, talking loudly and getting a 'wedgy' from a bunch of jocks in a car park. There's plenty of all three in this establishment because this is Rugger Bugger Central, where if you're not wearing the Rugby Regimentals – chinos, Dubes, Ralph and a sailing jacket – they'll look at you like you're wearing clogs and a leather codpiece. This is where D4's beautiful twenty-somethings kick back over a few Kens and discuss the big issues of the day: will Brian O'Driscoll still be playing for Leinster next season? Is the Nokia 8800 the greatest phone ever made? How did Amie-with-an-ie Drummond's tits suddenly get so big if she didn't have any? Signed rugby jerseys and photographs wainscot the walls, and you can barely make yourself heard over the sound of high-fiving and mobile phones ringing. The home ground of the Leinster team is just 100 yards from the front door and the players regularly show their faces for lunch or after matches, making Kielys as much a place of worship as a place of imbibing.

Despite its close proximity to St Vincent's Hospital, the **Merrion Inn** has never really attracted the famously warm-hearted nursey set. The M1, as *habitués* know it, is more a hangout for stuck-up UCD types, and, as far as scoring goes, you have to work hard for whatever you get. This place also attracts a lot of Andrew's and Michael's heads – in other words, people who left St Andrew's College or St Michael's College years ago, but talk about it like they're still there – rugger buggers enjoying a brief sabbatical from Kielys, and a rich, camel-hair-coated, fifty-something, empty-vessel stereotype known as Merrion Man.

The Schoolhouse is an old school building next to the canal in Ballsbridge, which has been tastefully converted into a four-star hotel. Its bar has become a favourite after-work hangout for South City suits who never had time to find a life partner. This is the place where D4 love stories – or at least marriages of convenience – begin. On Thursday and Friday nights it's quite a scene. You meet a girl, you exchange views on the privatization of Aer Lingus and suddenly you're loosening your tie. Six months later you're announcing your merger in the social pages of *The Irish Times*.

On the day of a big rugby international it's safe to drink just about anywhere within a mile of Lansdowne Road, provided, of course, you can put up with the back-slapping, *esprit de corps* and grown men calling each other by their surnames. Most fans enjoy their 'one or two' pre-match 'scoops' in Ballsbridge, choosing one of the drinking emporiums along a strip that non-rugby types refer to as Wankers Way. It includes famous 'battle cruisers' like **Paddy Cullen's**, **Crowe's**, **The Horse Show House** and, further up the street, **Bellamy's**. Rugby fans can be trusted to take their glasses out onto the street without sticking them in each other's faces, so when the weather's fine – which it always is in this sun-kissed part of the world – the match-goers spill outside, where the banter and bonhomie, to say nothing of jolly japery, can reach ear-splitting levels.

Here, too, you'll have the opportunity to leer at literally hundreds of young women in figure-hugging Ireland rugby jerseys. Interestingly, Umbro has never brought out a fitted Ireland soccer shirt for women – maybe because when you weigh 15 stone, *every* shirt is figure-hugging.

At the other end of the street, in the Four Seasons Hotel, is the impossibly glamorous **Ice Bar**, which combines the cosmopolitan sophistication of New York with the design cool of Milan and the bar prices of Dublin – in the year 2041. This is the home of the €6 bottle of Bud and the pint of Heino for €6.40. Try the €19 Champagne Mojito. It takes fifteen minutes to prepare, and they crush the ice and fresh mint right before your eyes. The regulars here – perfectly toned men in €2,000 suits and emaciated model-types with the signature D4 dead-fish stare – aren't afraid to look you up and down when you walk through the door. And don't worry about what to wear – no matter what you hang on yourself, you're going to feel completely under-dressed in here.

The King of Clubs

Dublin 4 men of a certain age love being members of clubs – as long as they are exclusive clubs. It's as vital to their sense of self as are the letters after their name. Possibly the only thing they enjoy more than being members of clubs is being on the **membership committees** of clubs, thus deciding who gets in and who doesn't, which allows them to enjoy the sweet power of veto over Cabinet ministers, high-court judges and captains of industry. There can be no greater trip than telling rich and powerful men to **fock off**. Most of the clubs in South Dublin have no waiting lists, and no criteria for membership are ever published. Not even the Consistory in Rome applies this much secrecy to its considerations, with nepotism and score-settling often playing a large part in the process.

Most D4 men are members of two clubs: one golf and one tennis/fitness club. There's very little mixing and matching – usually it's either Milltown Golf Club and Fitzwilliam Lawn Tennis Club, or it's Elm Park Golf Club and Riverview.

Milltown and **Elm Park** are Dublin 4's favourite golf courses (despite the fact that both are technically outside the postal district), and on an average weekend you'll find the entire Supreme Court, Law Library, boards of the major banks, most of the country's leading surgeons and all the important movers-and-shakers in Irish financial, legal and medical life traversing their fairways, looking like a tit in **ridiculous knitwear**.

The K Club might be more expensive and **Powerscourt** more prestigious, but Milltown and Elm Park can claim moral superiority over them for one reason – they are not impressed by money. Some of the country's wealthiest builders would give their left vestibules to become members, but, despite their billions, Ireland's new aristocracy have not been able to buy their way into either club. In fact, for whom is Michael Smurfit's golfing Elysium built if not for rich men who couldn't get into Milltown and Elm Park?

Nonetheless, the two clubs draw sneers from 'true' golfers – usually those they've blackballed at some point in the past – who assert vigorously that if it's not 7,000 yards long and next to the sea, then it's not a 'real' course. That's why most members of Milltown and Elm Park are also members of **Portmarnock Golf Club**. You'll often hear them explain: 'I play my *serious* golf in Portmornock – and my *social* golf in Elm Pork.'

Yes, it's heavy-duty banter in the Berkeley Court bar.

At **Fitzwilliam** you can play tennis or squash, enjoy a swim, or work off a carvery lunch in the steamroom or sauna, although FLTC has always regarded itself as more of a private gentlemen's club than a common leisure centre. The age profile of its membership – they seem to have more sixty-somethings than fifty-somethings these days – has seen it dubbed 'God's Waiting Room', or **the Devil's Waiting Room**, depending on your political viewpoint. The club, which grew out of a rundown shack on Lad Lane into its current, state-of-the-art headquarters on upmarket Appian Way, has always had an enlightened attitude towards minorities, accepting Jewish members at a time when virtually no other club in Ireland would do so. However, in the corner of the bar you can still find choleric old men bitching into their pints about the decision to allow **women** in.

Membership of **Riverview** – or David Lloyd Riverview Leisure – is more than just a line on your *Who's Who* entry, although obviously it's that as well. Located between Donnybrook and Clonskeagh, this prestigious club has a swimming pool, tennis courts and a very impressive gym, where you'll find the stars of the various schools Senior Cup teams eye-balling each other across the weights room as they work out between matches. Most of them are there because 'the old man' is a member, even though the last time he held a tennis racquet, Arthur Ashe had just won Wimbledon.

Botox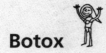

Dublin 4 girls are famous for their **inscrutable** faces. It's often impossible to gauge what mood they're in by simply looking at them. This is often the result of **Botox** injections, which freeze the face into a stony *moue*. However, by knowing the subtle nuances to look out for, it is possible to read a Dublin 4 girl's facial expressions. For a handy guide see pages 166–7.

Mount Anville

It's not, strictly speaking, in Dublin 4, but Mount Anville is where Dublin's richest mommies and daddies send their little **princesses** to be educated. It is the closest thing Dublin has to a **finishing school**, and its students – the celebrated 'Mounties' – graduate with not just an excellent education but also the confidence that comes from being well versed in

'Manolos! Manolos! Manolos!'

'What do you mean my credit cord has been refused? Oh my God, you are SO getting sued.'

'Oh my God, Fiachra wants me! And he's on, like, the first team!'

'I can't believe I ate that strawberry. I actually need to purge.'

'I'm grateful to you, fellow motorist, for letting me out of that side-street.'

'Sophie knew I liked that strapless dress in Morgan. She is SUCH a bitch, even though she's, like, my best friend and everything?'

'I'm having an orgasm!'

'I'm faking an orgasm.'

etiquette and all matters of **social refinement**.

This elite, fee-paying school, situated in the former home of railway tycoon William Dargan, has traditionally excelled at hockey, tennis, debating and drama, but extracurricular activities also include such urbane pursuits as furniture restoration. Mounties come across as fancying themselves – but then, everyone fancies *them*. Impossibly cool and trend-setting, they were the first girls' school to adopt **Dubes** as part of their uniform.

It is a well-kept secret – and one that students of nearby Alexandra and Muckross colleges will delight in – that Mount Anville was once on the **Northside**, starting out life in Glasnevin in 1853, before transferring to a better neighbourhood on the other side of the city in 1865.

The Society of the Sacred Heart, which founded and still runs the school, has five aims: to instil in its students a living faith in God; to encourage personal growth in an atmosphere of 'wise freedom'; to foster a deep respect for intellectual values; to stimulate the building of community as a Christian value; and to cultivate social awareness that 'impels to action'. Its students, on the other hand, have one aim: to get off with as many boys from **Blackrock College** as possible, or whoever happens to be doing well in the Leinster Schools Senior Cup. And, as their rivals know only too well, the Mounties *always* get their man.

A WORD FROM OISINN

I remember this one time we were all in Kielys after we had kicked somebody-or-other's orse in the Cup – I think it was, like, Michael's – and the place was just full of birds, all of them there for one reason alone – to try to be with anyone connected with our team. I shit you not, it was like conducting interviews. Anyway, I'd just red-corded this bird from, like, Teresians, of all schools, when suddenly next up is this absolute focking stunner – not my type, in other words!

She turned around to me and she went, 'Congrats – you'd a great game,' the usual opener for ten, and naturally I responded with, 'Thanks. So . . . what school do you go to?' expecting her to say, like, Mount Anville, or Alex, or Loreto Foxrock, or Muckross, or whatever. But no, totally out of the blue she went, 'John Scottus'.

So I was like, 'Can I ask you to say that again?'

'John Scottus,' she went and suddenly I'm having one of those tumbleweed moments. I do remember thinking that Scottus sounded like one of those infections that requires a dose of penicillin and two weeks out of the saddle. I think I might have actually mentioned this to her because it was at that point that she – not me – walked away.

So I asked around and it turns out that John Scottus is this, like, seriously exclusive school on Morehampton Road and the bird I knocked back – Sive was her name – has a dad who's worth, like, four billion squids and she now plays the violin – get this – for a living.

I stuck with what I knew and ended up with one of the harem of Mounties that attached itself to us that year. No regrets, though. They were great, those girls – like a flock of turquoise flamingos that followed us everywhere. Me, Ross and JP went through them like an epidemic. We used to have this joke: how many Mounties does it take to change a lightbulb? Four – one to go and get Daddy and the other three to bitch about her behind her back!

Anyway, if you asked me to choose a ladies' fragrance that captures the essence of Dublin 4, it would have to be *L'Eau d'Issey* by Issey Miyake. It's fresh and feminine, without being too flowery; unmistakable and persuasive, yet subtle and classically elegant. It's the perfect scent for an independent woman who's not afraid to express herself.

Entertainment

Dublin 4 dwellers love watching sport – especially from the vantage of a corporate box or sponsor's tent.

Lansdowne Road is the home of rugby, the arena in which Ireland have pulled off many famous victories and many equally famous defeats. The stadium – the oldest rugby union Test venue in the world – is due to

The morning after the night before! Before it closed for redevelopment, Lansdowne Road hosted occasional 'soccer' matches and, traditionally, supporters showed their gratitude by pissing in local gardens. Here, a housekeeper and gardener make their way in to work . . .

face the wrecking ball, with a new €700m, 40,000-seater stadium to be built in its place. The battered old stands have borne witness to a lot of history – Ireland winning the Triple Crown in 1982, coming seconds away from putting Australia out of the World Cup in 1991 and denying England the Grand Slam in 2001. (Regrettably, the stadium hosted occasional games of 'soccer', too, and thousands of men with newsprint moustaches laid siege to what is a quiet residential area, drinking cider, eating punnets of chips and shitting in local gardens.) During the stadium's reconstruction Ireland is playing its matches on the Northside of Dublin in a stadium called Crock Park. There are doubts about whether any Ireland fans – or players for that matter – will be able to find it. Thank Christ for Sat-Nav.

Not many people can say they have two homes in Dublin 4, but the **Leinster** rugby team can. They play their home games in the European Cup at the RDS and Celtic League games – a kind of European Cup Lite – in Donnybrook. The highlight of matches at the RDS is when the theme tune from *Hawaii Five-O* is played over the tinny public address system every time Leinster score a try.

The Dublin Horse Show is one of the highlights of the Dublin 4 social calendar, when ladies who wouldn't know their horses from their elbows don summer frocks and spectacular Philip Treacy millinery creations and feign knowledge and interest in showjumping. The real aficionados at the event, which takes place over five days in early August, are the boggers, who relegate the locals, for once, to the role of *arrivistes*. Still, as long as they have a plentiful supply of strawberries, a full flute of Champagne and good seats for the Aga Khan, the locals really don't mind. Merrion Cricket Club and Belvedere Rugby Club are among the local clubs which, in a display of ecumenism, allow their grounds to be used as car parks for the horse-trailer trash.

Since it first threw open its doors in 1975, **Funderland** has brought some of the world's scariest amusement rides to Ireland – and some of the world's scariest people into the heart of Dublin 4. The funfair, which operates out of the RDS from St Stephen's Day until the second week in January each year, attracts tens of thousands of poor people to Ballsbridge, many of them wearing soccer jerseys and sovereign rings. Dublin 4 thought it had seen the last of their kind when Shamrock Rovers, a soccer club, stopped playing matches in the RDS showjumping arena. A growing number of Southsiders – including Ross O'Carroll-Kelly's old dear and a couple of her friends – have come to regard Funderland's famous big wheel as a blot on the Dublin 4 skyline and are campaigning for the entire operation to be shifted **some place more appropriate**, which basically means Ballymun.

The RDS (Royal Dublin Society) was founded in 1731 by the philosophical society at Trinity College as a means of promoting arts, agriculture, industry and science in Ireland. The Move Funderland to the Northside pressure group say they fail to see what the famous funfair contributes in any of those three areas.

A WORD FROM CHRISTIAN

The rides in Funderland are supposed to be, like, scary, but they've never freaked me out, not even the Wall of Death.
I mean, what speed does that get up to? 100 ks an hour? A traditional Landspeeder – take Luke Skywalker's first SoroSuub X-34, for example – can hit 250 ks at top speed. I am not bullshitting you.

You think that's good? Remember those repulsorlift speeder bikes that the Empire used as, like, reconnaissance vehicles on Endor? Really put your foot down on one of those and the needle will start tipping 500 ks. Seriously, it'd make anything they have in Funderland look like a sandcrawler. But then, they're all in the ha'penny place compared to the scimitar assault bomber, which is, like, the new generation of TIE fighter. I heard this, like, rumour that this goy made the trip to hyperspace in one? We're talking light-speed velocity? Could be total bullshit, of course, but I believe it . . .

'Don't even get me onto Iron Maiden, Slipknot and Metallica,' spokeswoman Fionnuala O'Carroll-Kelly said during the group's annual Christmas picket of the RDS in 2006.

Other Highlights of Dublin 4

Kielys of Donnybrook serves a cocktail called the **Die Hard Brennan**, named after the Toulouse and former Ireland lock Trevor Brennan. This little concoction contains, appropriately enough, black and blue vodka, Curaçao, After Shock and orange juice, and its effect is just like being hit by the 18-stone man-mountain – in a juggernaut cab.

On Saturday and Sunday afternoons in Ballsbridge you can watch gangs of muscle-bound jocks, buzzing on Red Bull and creatine, throwing rugby balls around **Herbert Park**, watched by a chorusline of fawning females. It's an elaborate seduction ritual that's as old as rugby itself, and it's well worth a look.

Our Lady Queen of Peace Catholic Church on Merrion Road is one of the only church car parks in the world where clamping is in operation. You might think you're being clever lashing the Volvo in there instead of the pay-and-display car park at the front of the church before nipping into Bianconi's for a vanilla latte, but you are sure to incur the wrath of God's Clampers.

RTÉ screens a soap opera based in North Dublin called *Fair City*, which many Southsiders thought was a comedy for the first two years of its broadcast, designed to poke fun at their cousins across the river. Because of security considerations, the show is filmed not on location in the north inner city but in the **RTÉ car park** in Donnybrook, where a replica model of a typical Northside shithole has been built out of plywood. A visit to 'Carrickstown' is a great opportunity to view the shocking conditions in which these people live without having to actually cross the Liffey.

Sandymount has that most South Dublin of accoutrements, a yoga studio called **Exhale**, while **Browne's** coffee shop is one of the best places in Dublin 4 to ogle good-looking women over the top of your *Irish Times* Weekend section on a Saturday morning.

The excellent Terroirs in Donnybrook stocks not only fancy wine but **Michel Cluizel chocolate**, the most sure-fire way of getting into a girl's knickers short of telling her that you love her.

The French Paradox is a warm and Parisian-mannered wine-bar-cum-restaurant in Ballsbridge, which hosts **tastings** on Tuesday evenings. A couple of hours of tuition, a bellyful of vino and all the cheese and charcuterie you can stuff in your pockets – all for less than fifty sheets. It's a classy joint – *ooh la la* meets la di dah.

Suggested Itinerary in Dublin 4

Enjoy a hearty, traditional English breakfast at the
Berkeley Court Hotel. Take a taxi to Dublin Castle in the
City Centre to see a D4 denizen evade questions
relating to the source of his wealth at one of Ireland's
many tribunals of investigation. Go to Donnybrook Fair,
then take a picnic of linseed bread, Tallegio and quails'
eggs to Herbert Park. Realize you don't like Tallegio or
quails' eggs and don't care much for linseed bread
either. Dump all three in a bin. Watch the rugby stars of
tomorrow in action in a live Leinster Senior Schools Cup
match at Donnybrook. Enjoy the legendary 'one or two'
Kens in Kielys, followed by one or two Die Hard
Brennans. Phone the concierge at the Four Seasons in
Ballsbridge and ask him to send a limo for you. Check
into a suite. Enjoy dinner in the hotel restaurant.
Afterwards, order Champagne Mojitos for everyone in
the Ice Bar. Put it all on your credit card. Sell a kidney or
other non-vital internal organ to pay for it.

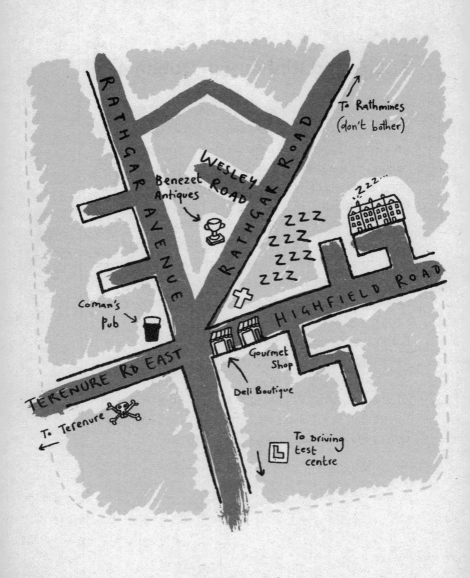

2. Rathgar

Rathgar – or Rath Gawr, as it's more popularly known – is South Dublin's **Left Bank**, a smug, sophisticated little suburb where there is no greater pleasure in the world than strolling down to one of the many local patisseries for an almond croissant or a poppy-seed baguette on a lazy Saturday morning. This is the place where many of Ireland's *über*-rich have found contentment and the quiet life. Rathgar is **one of the most boring places on Earth**, with hardly anything ever happening here – and that suits the locals just fine . . .

Rathmines is a student ghettoland, where nobody who has ever done a day's work, doesn't enjoy KFC or has no opinion on George W Bush, is safe at night.

High property prices and a more settled community have prevented Rathgar from becoming a student ghettoland like nearby Rathmines. A standard, semi-detached house in Rathgar will set you back about €1.5 million, or upwards of €2.5 million for a pile on one of Rathgar's famous **red-brick Victorian terraces**. Many of the stars of the Law Library have made their homes here, though most of Rathgar's wealth is inherited and old money snobbery abounds, so much so that plans are at an advanced stage to build an **Israeli-style security wall** to protect it from *arriviste* Terenure.

Rathgar is where most of South Dublin's rich kids go to fail their driving test – usually in their mothers' Fiat Puntos or Honda Civics. However, it's probably most synonymous with the takeaway gourmet food shops that have earned Rathgar the nickname **New Deli**.

The people of Rathgar are famous for their **snootiness and lack of sociability**, yet they are acutely aware of their place in the world. And if they're not, there are reminders everywhere. The dry cleaners in the village advertise their ironing service with giant pictures of Ralph Lauren and Tommy Hilfiger shirts in their window, while the local travel agents advertise holidays in some of the world's most exclusive ski resorts, shopping breaks in New York and long weekends in the foreign property supermarket of Dubai, which is known as the Rathgar of the East. The village even boasted its own **piano shop**, though it recently relocated to a site just off the M50 as just about everybody in Rathgar already owns a Steinbach, Viscount or Rodgers.

Visitors to Rathgar will discover a contented, leafy idyll that's as somnolent as a sunny Sunday morning in June.

History

Rath is the Gaelic word for 'revenge', while *Gar* means 'rich people'. Shortly after the failed 1798 rebellion the area was settled by a group of wealthy landowners and businessmen, who wanted to put distance between themselves and the uncouth element north of the Liffey, and were ignorant enough to think they **could live without the English.** Most Rathgar residents can trace their ancestral lineage back to that seminal moment in the village's history.

Rathgar has always had a large, **well-to-do Protestant population**. It's interesting that it's the Presbyterian church, Christ Church, at the junction of Rathgar Road and Highfield Road that dominates the village. The less imposing Church of the Three Patrons on Rathgar Road was historically known as **the servants' church**, as most of the Catholics in the town were only there to clean people's houses. Happily, this is one of the fine traditions that has been preserved to

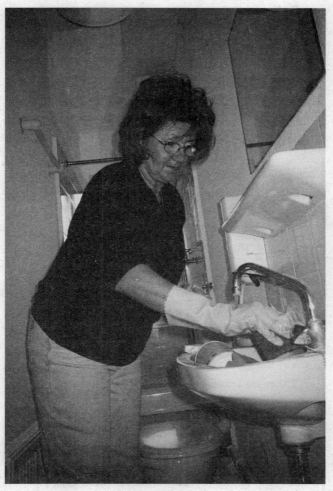

South Dublin's slaves were freed by the Emancipation Act of 1998, though many chose to remain in servitude, knowing no other way of life.

this day, though most of Rathgar's 'domestics' have been moved out of their old mews quarters and into nearby Rathmines and Harold's Cross.

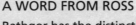

A WORD FROM ROSS

Rathgor has the distinction of being one of the seven test centres where I've, like, failed my driving test. I think they might even have put up a plaque to say that. Looking back, roysh, this was the one I felt most confident about passing. I actually did a serious amount of cramming the night before and even, like, drove the route a couple of times? So I turn up for the test, roysh, and it turns out I went out on a couple of dates with the examiner's daughter, Elmarie. Not good news. But I suppose when you've been around the track more times than *Beef or Salmon*, these things are bound to happen.

I have bad memories of driving both of them, as it happens.

I was out with Elmarie one night, coming back from the flicks, I think, when she turned around to me and said those seven deadly words: 'I don't believe in sex before marriage.' It was probably a bit horsh, roysh, but I put her out of the cor. Don't worry, I did actually stop first.

Anyway, roysh, her old man obviously knows who I am and he knows my rep, because from the time we set off he was giving me majorly negative vibes. I mean, he ended up failing me for pretty much nothing. Except those two near-crashes, only one of which was my fault, I might add. Anyway, roysh, at the end he tells me to return to the test centre and I'm sensing the dude's hostility and I'm thinking, Hey, all this aggravation ain't satisfactioning me, Dude. So I end up putting him out of the cor as well. Maybe he was going to give me a pass after all. Still, it was worth it to see his face when he was standing at the focking bus stop.

Famous Residents

James Joyce was born in Rathgar, in Brighton Square, so it's well he could afford to swan off to Paris to write books that no one can understand. Another famous author, **Bram Stoker**, lived in Orwell Park in the later part of his life. His book about a man with slicked-back hair who dresses in black and sucks blood out of people is believed to be based on his experiences with South Dublin estate agents. **Jack Lynch**, Ireland's former Taoiseach, lived in Rathgar for a time and is believed to be the only GAA player ever to do so, while the murdered underworld figure **Martin Cahill** – *aka* The General – lived at Cowper Downs . . . a bit too close to Rathgar for the liking of many locals.

A WORD FROM FIONN

John Millington Synge, the dramatist and poet, grew up in Rathgar. He was actually born in Rathfarnham, but when he was young his father died from smallpox and he moved with his mother to Rathgar, to the house next door to his maternal grandmother. He is said to have developed his lifelong love of ornithology while studying the birds along the banks of the River Dodder. His masterpiece, of course, was *The Playboy of the Western World*, which was first performed at the Abbey in 1907 and caused riots because of its portrayal of peasant life in rural Ireland.

Which is interesting . . .

Shopping

Not a huge amount. Rathgar is one of those villages where there's a lot less to it than meets the eye. That's fine by the locals, who don't want it turned into some kind of bazaar. **Lamps and Lighting** is a seriously swanky shop, where you can buy lights that will – get this – determine the mood of each room in your house. Then there's the wonderful **Benezet Antiques**, a real Aladdin's Cave of a shop where you can pick up everything from an early-twentieth-century dresser for €8,500 to a Victorian-style coal scuttle for less than €1,000.

How to Get There

Rathgar is well served by public transport, with a number of routes linking it not only to Dublin City Centre but also to the suburbs of Terenure, Templeogue and Tallaght. We are unable to publish details of these routes, however, due to the threat of a court injunction by the people of Rathgar.

Where to Eat

At home. See below.

'I'll take that to go' ⊜

Rathgar isn't terribly well served by coffee shops where you can spend a couple of hours dawdling over an espresso mallowchino or an orange and passionfruit infusion, catching up on the local gossip. Rathgar folk like to keep themselves to themselves, and even the ladies-who-lunch prefer to do so at home in their expensive chrome-and-glass fitted kitchens. This explains why Rathgar has more **delicatessens** and **gourmet food shops** per head of population than Greenwich Village. In fact, so synonymous has it become with creamy puy lentils, mozzarella tartlets and spinach, roast pepper and feta quiche that Rathgar regularly tops internet polls to find **Ireland's gayest town**.

With its blue-and-white striped awning swaying gently in the breeze, **Deli Boutique** reflects the Parisian pretensions of its customers, who flock there on Saturday and Sunday mornings to buy croissants and *pain au chocolat* for their eleven o'clock brunch.

Perusing the shelves of the excellent **Gourmet Shop** will have you feeling like you've just stepped into the pages of a Famous Five book – fennel bread, avocados and, of course, lashings of ginger beer, not to mention other essentials, such as Rooibosch tea, organic tofu and *riso arborio*.

Even people who live alone are well catered for, with **The Butler's Pantry** stocking a wide range of ready-cooked meals-for-one in little aluminium trays. Sad? Well, how does gravadlax sound to you – apart from **impossibly foreign**? Or how about ricotta, leek and pinenut strudel followed by smoked trout and salmon timbales? With a menu like that, who needs a wife? In fact, the duck rillette with balsamic onions and orange is considered the main reason why Rathgar's twenty- and thirty-somethings are choosing not to marry.

A WORD FROM OISINN
If you were to ask me to choose a ladies' fragrance that captures the essence of Rathgar, I would probably have to go for *Classique* by Jean Paul Gaultier. It's mild and vanilla-sweet, yet has an impossible elusiveness and an indefinable mystique.

Pubs and Clubs

Coman's is where Rathgar's young, well-heeled set hang out, a pub that looks like it's been torn from the pages of a Habitat catalogue, with **big red chairs** and **mood lighting** everywhere, not to mention a wine

shop. Around here they even prefer their drink
'to go'.

Entertainment

Coman's has a toilet with a **sensor-operated flushing
action**.

Suggested Itinerary in Rathgar

Go to a deli, buy a chocolate croissant and eat it
standing outside one of the big swanky houses on
Victoria Road or Zion Road, imagining what it would be
like to live there. Buy *The Dubliner* magazine, the local
bible, and read it over a cappuccino while sitting in a
big red chair in Coman's. Sit your driving test. Buy an
expensive lamp. Bed by 2 pm.

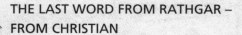

THE LAST WORD FROM RATHGAR – FROM CHRISTIAN

Rathgar is, like, cool. It's such a great place to go and kick back and chillax. Han and Leia took the kids there when all that shit was going down with the Koornacht Cluster ... oh, no, actually ... no, I'm thinking of Rathalay, which is this, like, planet that has these, like, grey basalt beaches? But where you can't swim because they're pretty dangerous, those waters. See, they've got, like, narkaas, which would basically chew you in half. The number of people who've been eaten while diving for mote shells, you wouldn't actually believe ...

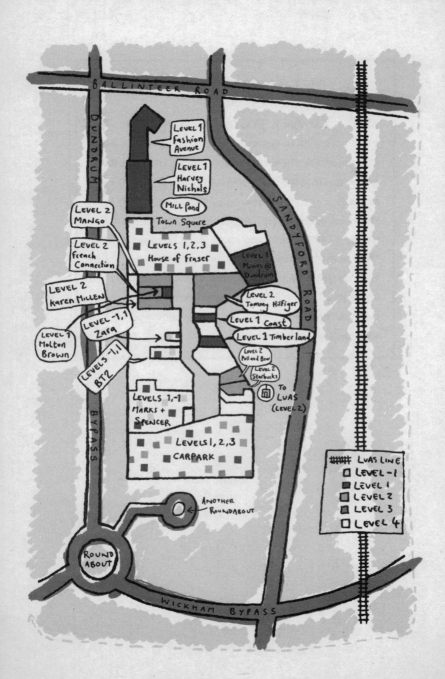

3. Dundrum

It would be wrong to describe Dundrum as a village. It's so much less than that. It's a **big shopping centre** with some houses around it. But then, to refer to Dundrum Town Centre as a shopping centre is to sell it woefully short – it's the quintessential South Dublin lifestyle experience. It's so stuffed to the oxters with marquee-name shops, cafés and restaurants, you could pass a whole day and night in here without ever knowing it – and with no clocks and very few windows onto the outside world, it's quite possible you will . . .

South Dublin is where you'll see clothes associated with vastly different climatic regions – on the same body. These famous fleece-lined Ugg boots, for instance, are usually worn with short skirts, strappy tops and a litre or two of fake tan. From the knees up, you're going nightclubbing in Rio de Janeiro. From the knees down, you're going seal-clubbing in Antarctica.

Set in the heart of the self-styled Dublin 4 (teen), this is where the Celtic Tiger cubs go to dispose of their income. Seven days a week, twenty-four hours a day, they keep the **tills ringing**. This is mall life as South Dublin's close friends, the Americans, live it, with thousands of people thronging the well-oxygenated, artificially lit atria, shopping intently or simply 'hanging out'.

Here, you'll see women in their forties in jodhpurs and tight white shirts, with dyed blonde hair and all-year tans, flashing **fake smiles** at shop assistants who

194

look like they don't really need to work. You'll see red-faced men in **Pringle sweaters**, laden down with shopping bags, tagging along after them and conducting conversations at impossibly high decibel levels on their mobile phones. However, most of its *habitués* are under the age of twenty-five, predominantly sixteen- and seventeen-year-old girls with bodies like nine-year-old Chinese gymnasts, wearing UGG boots, mini-skirts and expertly applied fake tan. And teenage boys with blond streaks, wearing pink Airtexes or Leinster rugby shirts. In short, everyone is happy, beautiful – and carrying a large **coffee**, **fruit juice** or **smoothie** 'to go'.

Check out the cars in Dundrum's state-of-the-art 'smart-park'. It's full of 07 BMWs, VW Beetle convertibles and people-carriers built like Panzer tanks – a perfect snapshot of a contented, materialistically happy Ireland at the dawn of a new century.

History

Dundrum was a dull South Dublin suburb famous for its **traffic congestion** and its **psychiatric hospital**. A planning application was lodged to build a shopping centre with almost 100,000,000 square feet of retail space. It was built. South Dublin lived **happily ever after**.

A WORD FROM ROSS
Dundrum is the site of Ireland's first ever Storbucks, the world's greastest coffee shop, which I – like basically millions of other South Dubliners – fell in love with while I was in the States, on a J1er. I was, like, never out of the one in Ocean City. Even when I hadn't got two cents to my name, I knew I could always go in there for a tall white chocolate mocha and a peach and raspberry muffin, roysh, and stick them on the old man's AmEx cord. It's something I still do to this day . . . although it's his Visa I have now.

Famous Residents

Oh, a few names you might have heard of: Harvey Nichols? Karen Millen? Tommy Hilfiger? How about Paul Rankin? Or Hugo Boss? Ernest Jones, anyone? Toni & Guy?

Shopping

Is the Pope Catholic? There's House of Fraser, Marks & Spencer, Harvey Nichols and a Tesco that's open twenty-four hours a day. For his and hers 'clobber' there's BT2, Pull and Bear, Timberland, Tommy Hilfiger, Coast, Esprit, French Connection, G-Star, Karen Millen, Lacoste, Mango and Zara. There's Molton Brown and their famous fine liquid handwash. Women will be happy to hear that there are sixteen shoe shops under Dundrum's roof, including Fitzpatricks, Office and Schuh. And guys, if the blissful, child-in-a-sweetshop atmosphere induces in you an urge to pop the question, there are eight jewellers' windows to stare into while she's putting the Manolos on your Mastercard. Penneys, H&M, Argos and Champion Sports are also here – if you're into that kind of thing.

How to Get There

Across broken glass on your hands and knees if you have to! Fortunately, that's not strictly necessary, as Dublin Bus operates a large number of routes that service Dundrum, including the **14, 14A, 17, 44, 48A, 48N** and **75**. The Luas also stops right outside, though remember that Balally Station is two minutes' closer to the shopping centre than Dundrum Station. And you will want every one of those precious seconds when you step into this consumerist wonderland.

Yummy-Drummies

Yummy-Drummies are Dundrum's own indigenous female population. They're between fourteen and seventeen years of age, with pencil-thin bodies, baggy clothes, messy hair and perfect make-up. They move in packs of between four and eight, very slowly and in a triangle, between BT2, Boost and Starbucks, sucking smoothies up a straw, texting while they walk, and **hugging** and **air-kissing** each other in a very insincere manner.

Their 'look' – scratcher *chic* – is inspired by glossy magazine images of stars like Jessica Simpson and Lindsay Lohan caught by the paps nipping out for a carton of milk and a packet of fags in a big, sloppy jumper on a Saturday morning. They all dress identically, having chosen their clothes for the day only after long, tortuous hours of consultation with each other through text messaging. Generally, it's over-sized hooded sweatshirts, sloppy, shapeless tracksuit bottoms and either **UGG boots** or **Dubes**. Occasionally they'll wear mini-skirts, though that too will have been decided by 'SMS Democracy in Action'.

The petulant look is in right now, and Yummy-Drummies are famous for having the sulkiest pouts in Western Europe, enhanced by tubes of collagen-effect

lip plumper. The hair is worn just-out-of-bed messy.
Yummy-Drummies will spend on average one hour in
front of the mirror trying to make their hair look like
they haven't touched it at all. The application of

make-up and fake tan is a slow, meticulous process, as painstaking as excavating an archaeological site, but involving **more brushes**.

 ### A WORD FROM OISINN
My cousin, Noni, she's a Yummy-Drummy. She went shopping with her old dear a while back and they got separated when they ran into basically three groups of Yummy-Drummies coming from different directions – we're talking *The Perfect Storm* here.

So when the smoke clears, Noni's old dear doesn't know which kid is hers – they all look the focking same. So she ends up grabbing this one who, in fairness, was wearing a very similar navy Abercrombie hoody, tight jeans and UGGs, and she brings her home. It's five days before she realizes she's got the wrong kid! This one's called Abby or some shit. Anyway, she wasn't going to say anything because I think Abby was actually bleeding less money out of her than Noni had been. More economical to run, I suppose. But it turned out Abby's old dear wanted her back.

If I had to choose a ladies' fragrance to capture the spirit of Dundrum, it would have to be *Happy* by Clinique – fresh, *chic*, modern and multi-layered.

Where to Eat

Like Tom Hanks's character in the movie *The Terminal*, you could spend twenty years of your life in Dundrum Town Centre and never get sick of the food. It's all here for you. And not just **Starbucks**. There's the **Bagel Factory**, **Brambles** and **BBs** for lunch; **Mao**, **Milano** and **Dunne & Crescenzi** for dins . . . and that's only the start of it. There's **Café Paul Rankin**, **Harvey Nicks** . . . Children could grow up here, happy and healthy. Come to think of it, they do.

A WORD FROM CHRISTIAN
Dundrum, yeah, it's like, big and shit? But it's nothing compared to Coruscant, which is this planet that's literally the centre of the universe and it's, like, totally a city, as in every square metre of it is covered in, like, skyscrapers and shit? And some of them are, like, a kilometre high. And there's, like, no roads? It's all, like, air traffic and shit? And it's got, like, the Grand Towers, the Skydome Botanical Gardens, the Galactic Museum and the Holographic Zoo of Extinct Animals, none of which Dundrum has. So . . . if you're, like, asking me which is better, I'd basically have to go with Coruscant.

Highlights of Dundrum

For starters, there's the 3,400-berth **car park** with state-of-the-art navigation system. A meter tells you how many parking spaces are available on each floor. All empty berths are lit up by a green light, which makes finding a parking space no effort at all. Forgotten where you left the 'jammer'? It doesn't matter. When you pulled into your space, your registration was photographed and logged in a computer. Find an information station, key in your reg and it'll tell you exactly where to find your car. If there is a heaven, these people will be in charge of the parking lot.

Movies@Dundrum is Dundrum Town Centre's very own cinema, with big, comfy chairs and a total of twenty screens. The only worry is whether Hollywood can make enough movies to keep them all open.

Knights Barber Shop is where the young jocks who've started sprouting facial hair go for a traditional wet shave with an open razor, which is currently all the rage in South Dublin.

There's also a **medical centre** that's equipped to deal with everything from bloodied noses picked up in the course of bargain-hunting to more severe cases of **shopper's remorse**.

A WORD FROM JP

I've been to Dundrum, once. Quite disappointed to discover that Veritas has no branch there yet, although Eason's has a pretty good spiritual living section.

Overall, though, I would have to say I was appalled by what I saw out there – a big orgy of consumption in which nobody was holding back. We have become such an acquisitive society, with people so desperate to get material things for their own sake.

We know from Luke 12:15: 'Jesus said to his disciples, "Watch out. Be on your guard against all kinds of greed; a man's life does not consist in the abundance of possessions." And he told them this parable: "The ground of a certain rich man produced a good crop. He thought to himself, What shall I do? I have no place to store my crops. Then he said, This is what I'll do. I will tear down my barns and build bigger ones, and there I will store all my grain and my goods. And I'll say to myself, You have plenty of good things laid up for many years. Take life easy; eat, drink and be merry. But God said to him, You fool! This night your life will be demanded from you. Then who will get what you have prepared for yourself? This is how it will be with anyone who stores up things for himself but is not rich towards God."'

Suggested Itinerary in Dundrum

Get up early. Go to Dundrum Town Centre. Stay until you're asked to leave.

In a 2007 survey on social and sexual attitudes in South Dublin, over 10,000 women were asked their favourite posititon – 67% said facing Harvey Nichols.

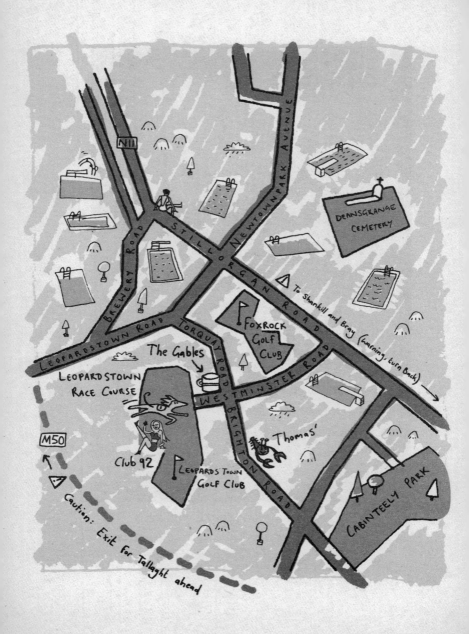

4. Foxrock

Foxrock. The Big Cohiba. Not so much a village as a community of obscenely wealthy people who have locked themselves into mansions behind enormous privet hedges and electric gates. It's often said that the rest of South Dublin is a purgatory for rich men awaiting their eternal reward in Foxrock – and that's truer than ever today. Home to businessmen, barristers, surgeons and literally thousands of **lady golfers**, Foxrock is the dream they try to sell you in the National Lottery ads, though the truth is you'd need to win **three roll-over jackpots** just to secure the deposit for a pad here. Houses in Foxrock aren't advertised for sale in estate agents' windows; they're sold at auction for sums resembling telephone numbers – with foreign prefixes . . .

All play and no work. In South Dublin, every hour is happy hour. Here, a couple enjoy a traditional Foxrock breakfast – a massive cocktail in a swimming pool.

Anyone who says money can't buy happiness should be forced to spend an afternoon sipping Gin Slings and eating organic chocolate noisettes while floating on a lilo in one of the heated **swimming pools** that grace the back of just about every property in this truly idyllic part of South Dublin. As far as life goes, the only handicap here is the one you're paying an instructor €200 an hour to help you lower.

Foxrock men aren't afraid to pick their noses at the wheels of their big German cars, and, thanks to a Special Amenity Area Order, Foxrock women are permitted to use their **mobile phones** while driving, safeguarding a tradition that stretches back since time immemorial. In fact, the name Foxrock, from the Gaelic *Carraig an tSionnaigh*, means 'women driving big Tourans while speaking on tiny Motorolas'.

Foxrock folk present a wonderfully paradoxical mix of superiority and insecurity, constantly measuring themselves and their worth against others, especially their nearest neighbours. Here, wealth is judged by the **Bedrooms-to-Children Index**, the average being 3:1.

Foxrock is such a prestigious address, it's not surprising that some have sought to confuse its borders. 'Real' Foxrock residents, in other words those with swimming pools, believe that only three roads – **Torquay**, **Brighton** and **Westminster** – are worthy of the name Foxrock and that the more affordable, semi-detached houses on the other side of the dual-carriageway should be redesignated Deansgrange West.

A visit to Foxrock is a wonderfully sobering experience. Even with ten grand in your pocket, you'll still feel like a pauper!

History

Foxrock has no roads named after republican heroes – dying for Ireland was always considered a terribly **working-class** idea here. Instead, its fragrant byways are named after either English towns where very, very wealthy people go to die (Torquay, Brighton) or the

British parliament (Westminster), which is still considered by many in Foxrock to be the **official seat of power** for Ireland. Similarly, the names of its houses reflect Foxrock's strong identification with Britain, with lots of references to Abbots and Friars and also former colonial outposts, such as Aden and Brahmapur.

Foxrock paid a price for its West Brit leanings, however. Kiltieragh, the home of Sir Horace Plunkett, was burnt down by republicans in 1923, which helps explain why, to this day, Sinn Féin polls so badly in Foxrock at election time.

A WORD FROM FIONN

Foxrock was the birthplace of Samuel Beckett, who happens to be one of my favourite writers. His novels and plays are bleak, minimalist and offer a pessimistic view of human nature, coloured by his own personal experiences, especially his fraught and ultimately unresolved relationship with his mother. His work was, in his own words, an art of impoverishment and failure. And yet alleviating that sense of fatalism is Beckett's dark and devious sense of humour, which lays bare the absurdity of human existence and our futile obsession with meaning.

Which is interesting ...

After Independence, Foxrock's landed gentry got on with the business of making potloads of cash. Modern Foxrock has a GNP equivalent to some of the world's leading corporations, though wealth has in no way softened them. These people love a fight. In the 1960s they succeeded in having the **Dublin Harcourt Street Line** closed down because the stop at Foxrock was drawing undesirables into the area to have what's known colloquially as 'a gawp'. And the fight continues, with hundreds of residents lining up to oppose the **extension of the Luas line** to Foxrock. A hard-hitting campaign, involving a charity ball and at least two fashion shows, has helped raise awareness of the potential horrors of public transport for a unique area like Foxrock.

Shopping 🍦

Foxrock is not exactly a shopper's paradise – the people here have Paris and Milan for that – but **Pace** is a shoe shop and **Lily** a boutique where many local ladies go to pick up something 'a bit different, very unusual'.

THE FFS

FFs – or Foxrock Fannies – refers to a type of woman indigenous to this corner of Dublin. Foxrock Fannies are typically in their forties or fifties and members of West Wood gym in Leopardstown, Carrickmines Croquet and Lawn Tennis Club and at least one golf club. Three mornings a week they perform an aerobic or Body Training System programme while wearing a full mask of make-up. Whether dressing up or down, they always strive to look their best, to the point of accessorizing their tracksuits. They never, ever wash their own hair, instead having it shampooed and set four times a week, usually in The Lounge, the local beauty salon where one can hear the loud exclamations of 'You . . . look . . . fab-a-lous!' from as far away as Cabinteely.

FFs speak with a flat, nasal timbre and bitch about their housekeepers over coffee with their friends – 'the girls' – in the Gables two or three mornings a week.

They all have little yappy dogs. They enjoy organizing fund-raising functions, such as cocktail balls and golf outings, but only if there's kudos to be had from them.

Their children are mostly reared, with their

youngest well into secondary school – fee-paying, naturally. Their husbands are semi-retired professionals, and they have holiday homes, and golf club memberships abroad, mostly in Villamoura.

One characteristic of Foxrock Fannies is that they never admit to planning holidays. They talk about 'nipping over' to the place in Portugal, as if it were a spur-of-the-moment thing. And oddly for women of such means, they love a bargain, especially a cheap flight.

It's a biological fact that Foxrock Fannies have no embarrassment gene. In shops they ask for discounts at full volume and make appointments to view houses for sale in the area, their only business being to pry.

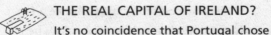 **THE REAL CAPITAL OF IRELAND?**
It's no coincidence that Portugal chose Westminster Park in Foxrock for the site of its Irish embassy. The Portuguese are so used to running into people from Foxrock – who've bought up most of Praia da Rocha – that most locals think Foxrock, not Dublin, is the capital of Ireland. And of course they're right.

How to Get There

In 1990, following a **forty-year stand-off** with CIÉ, local residents agreed to remove a series of barricades and allow a limited public transport service into Foxrock.

Under an agreement hammered out between locals and the company, just one single **86** passes along Brighton Road, at 7.25 am, on weekday mornings only. There are also a limited number of **63** buses permitted to drive through old Foxrock. Meanwhile, the **mortgage-paying classes** who live east of the dual-carriageway have access to any number of bus routes, including the **46A**, **84** and the **145**.

A WORD FROM OISINN

Of course, Loreto Foxrock is the school for birds out that direction. I suppose, like the rest of the goys, I broke a fair few horts out there in my time, especially when we put on *West Side Story* with them in, like, transition year. The school is opposite that massive church, Our Lady of Perpetual Succour – or Our Lady of Perpetual Sexual Frustration, as we used to call it.

There'd be a lot of lookers in there, though a lot of them have serious chips on their shoulders about not being sent to Mount Anville. After school they tend to hang around Stillorgan Shopping Centre, especially McDonald's, where seven or eight of them will sit around, like, one Diet Coke. There's a joke that the Macky D's in Stillorgan is the only one in the world operating at a loss.

A ladies' fragrance to sum up Foxrock? *Chanel No. 5*, of course – old, but yet timeless; sophisticated, decisive and with an uncompromising femininity.

Where to Eat

The Gables is known to serve the best Jerusalem artichokes and *mooli* in all of South Dublin, though it's probably best known as a hangout for Ladies Who Brunch. Check out the cars outside on a Saturday morning – XK8 Jag convertibles, Porsche Cayennes, X5 BMW jeeps. This is where the battle for the lady captaincy of the golf club is won or lost, and where some Olympic-standard bitching and back-stabbing takes place over Black Forest lattes and macadamia biscotti.

The Silken Glider overlooks the parade ring in

Dublin's only racecourse and is where Foxrock mommies and daddies take their little princesses to celebrate landmark occasions in their lives, such as eighteenth and twenty-first birthdays, Leaving Certificate results and **breaking in their first pair of Jimmy Choos**.

Thomas's, purveyors of fine food, is an institution in Foxrock. No one asks for jam here, they ask for wild blueberry preserve with a hint of lavender. Or goose fat. Or pink lemonade. Or wine with real **dust** on the bottle. Or a type of muesli that looks so like *pot-pourri* you won't know whether to eat it or put it in a bowl on top of the toilet cistern as an alternative to lighting matches.

Entertainment

Foxrock has its own variation of the turning on of the Christmas lights. On the first Friday night in December

the local ladies congregate in the village to show off their new **Da Vinci Veneers** – the brilliant-white ceramic caps they have fixed to their teeth at €700 apiece. On a count of three, they suddenly smile, creating a spectacular **flash in the night sky** that is said to be visible from as far away as Anglesey.

St Stephen's Day at Leopardstown Racecourse is when all of Foxrock comes out to show its plumage. There's an unofficial competition among the ladies for the best Philip Treacy-designed hat, while the men wager ostentatious bets, **almost always on the favourite**.

Finally, in the early hours of the morning, after Club 92 has shut its doors, there's the annual **Losing of the Virginity**, when girls half-cut on Smirnoff Ice and Bacardi Breezers have sex for the first time on the racecourse, while a crowd watching from the main stand shout her home. Later that day there's the lesser-known **Getting of the Morning-After Pill**, which tends to be an all-female affair.

Pubs and Clubs

Foxrock is famously the only village in Ireland without a pub, as they're considered even more working class than dying for Ireland. The nearby Leopardstown racecourse has a number of bars, however, the most popular of which is the slightly risqué-sounding Fillies. It's not, as the name might imply, wall to wall with girls

TWO VERY DIFFERENT VIEWS ON CLUB 92 FROM JP AND ROSS

 I always enjoyed Club 92. There's nothing wrong with dancing, of course. When David killed the Philistine, didn't the women of Israel greet King Saul with singing and dancing and joyful songs and tambourines and lutes?

'Let them praise His name with dancing.' That's Psalms 149:3, that is.

 Ninety-two. Knackery Doo. Shoot Your Goo. Call it what you like, but it's not for nothing that Club 92 is Dublin's official Club d'Amour. It's not your usual sweating hogpen, where mulchies in bogball jerseys go to bag off with nurses. There're no tight Levis and Ben Sherman shirts untucked in the Club of Love. No, this is the highest density of quality Blankers-Koen per square yord in the world, and the easiest place in Ireland to cop off with something decent on a Thursday or a Sunday night. Seriously goys, if you don't get it in there, you might as well take a blunt scissors to the thing.

of persuadable virtue, but rather a Continental-style café bar – the kind of place we'll all be drinking in if **Michael McDowell** has his way.

Then there's the world-famous **Club 92**. It holds 1,200 bodies, but women tend to outnumber men by a ratio of 2:1. You have to like those odds. When you pass under the iconic Club of Love sign and through those double doors, you'll feel like Brad Pitt. If you don't cop off in Club 92, the bouncers will give you a hug on the way out.

Other Highlights in Foxrock

At the **Leopardstown Golf Centre** you can perfect your drive, chip or putt – or why not just hang around the seventy-four-bay, floodlit driving range and watch men and women engage in **swinging**, Foxrock-style – complete with video cameras. In the pursuit of the perfect golf game, many Foxrock mommies and daddies go to the lengths of filming their swings, using a camcorder mounted on a tripod and connected to a laptop. Watch them quietly despair about their **'glitch at seven o'clock'**.

If you want to watch Foxrock folk really tearing their hair out, the QBC is the place to be. The Foxrock QBC – or **Quality Bus Corridor** – is a traffic lane reserved for buses and taxis only and runs from Foxrock Church right into Dublin City Centre. Foxrock's natural aversion towards public transport is turned into something approaching **road rage** by the sight of 46A after 46A tearing along wide, open road while they inch their Mercs and Jags forward in the gridlock.

Foxrock ladies love **charity events**, whatever the cause. Whether it's Roulades for Romania, Flans for Fibrosis or Cocktails for the Kidney Foundation, they can be relied upon to turn up en masse – provided, of course, that *VIP* or *Tatler* have a **photographer** there.

Suggested Itinerary in Foxrock

Stand on the Stillorgan dual-carriageway, just south of Foxrock church, and watch some of the biggest and most expensive cars in Ireland make the left turn off Westminster Road. Enjoy a brunch of Eggs Benedict on wheaten bread at the Gables, eavesdropping on Fionnuala, Delma and the girls as they compare body-balance programmes or discuss the likely contenders for the lady captain's prize. Walk up and down Westminster, Brighton and Torquay roads, admiring the homes of the fabulously rich through any gaps you can find in the privet hedges. Get arrested. Released around 10.00 pm. Bed.

FINALLY, A WORD TO THE UNWARY – FROM ROSS

There's, like, a lot of people, roysh, who claim to be from Foxrock when they're actually not. They're from, like, Carrickmines, Sandyford, Deansgrange, even as far away as Cornelscourt. They're, like, total impostors. Club 92 is full of them. I'm one of the chosen few who can put my hand on my hort and say, 'I'm actually from Foxrock,' except that if you are from Foxrock, it's considered, like, vulgar to say it. Even when you're giving your address, you just put Brighton Road or Torquay Road and then Dublin 18.

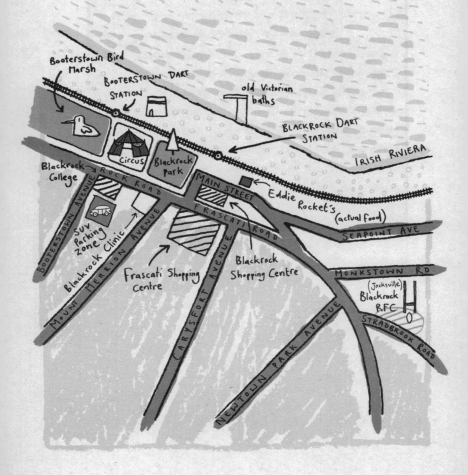

5. Blackrock & Booterstown

Hang on to your underpants – you are now entering Jockland! Blackrock and Booterstown were once described as being like a big piss-up in a rugby club bar. This is the home of the high-five, birthplace of drinking games like Mince Pies and Chariots of Fire, and the town that gave the world the atomic wedgy. But there's more to Blackrock and Booterstown than fun and games that can cause you to lose a testicle. As the site of Ireland's most prestigious secondary school, this region of South Dublin could be described as the **Cradle of the Celtic Tiger**, the area that turned out the brains that brought about Ireland's economic miracle . . .

Bob Geldof is, for many people, the quintessential South Dubliner, with his Blackrock College education, his highly conspicuous charity work and his penchant for telling people to fock off.

Blackrock is the birthplace of **Bob Geldof**, the site of Ireland's most exclusive hospital and the scene of some of the worst traffic congestion in the entire world. In fact, in 2004 a delegation of Mexican public officials looking for solutions to their capital's gridlock visited Blackrock, and then decided their traffic jams weren't so bad after all. They went home and spent their budget on a tequila theme park instead.

Blackrock's primary association is with **rugby**, however, and it has produced such famous names as Fergus Slattery, Neil Francis, Brendan Mullin and Brian O'Driscoll – and such imaginative nicknames as Slats,

Franno, Brenny and Drico. The people here are a wonderfully stuck-up lot. Young girls between the ages of eight and ten wear specially adapted neck braces to teach them how to walk with their **noses in the air**, while the Marks & Spencer in Blackrock has more yummy-mummies per square foot of retail space than any other outlet in Ireland or the United Kingdom.

Blackrock is also justly famous for having some of Dublin's most beautiful and historically important buildings **demolished** to make way for shopping centres and housing estates. Frescati House, the childhood home of Lord Edward FitzGerald, leader of the United Irishmen during the 1798 rebellion, is now the car park of the Frascati Centre, while Talbot Lodge, the nursing home where Éamon de Valera died, was bulldozed in the early 1990s to make room for more **big houses**.

The people here love to shop, and in Blackrock they have not one but two of the swankiest shopping centres anywhere in Ireland, not to mention Superquinn, with its world-famous **fresh bread**.

If you visit Blackrock, you'll get to see some of the brattiest children alive. Moms and dads in this part of the world think it's important for their children to **express themselves** – even if that means little Cillian screaming his lungs out while you quietly die of a hangover at the next table in any of the town's excellent coffee shops.

On the Blackrock seafront lie the dilapidated remains of the old Victorian swimming **baths**, whose high-diving board is one of the most famous features on the South Dublin skyline and a bleak reminder of an extinct civilization of poor people who once called Blackrock home. Happily, not any more. You'd be fortunate to find a decent house here for less than €1 or €2 million on a street with no satellite dishes.

History

Blackrock was originally called Newtown-on-the-Strand and was renamed Blackrock after the large **black rocks** that could be seen offshore at low tide. In medieval times, before Sandymount and Ballsbridge were settled, they marked the edge of the area controlled by the city of Dublin, in other words, the beginning of the Southside.

Booterstown means '**the town of the road**' – not the ugly, gridlocked one that cuts a swathe through it nowadays, but Slighe Cualann, one of the five great roads of ancient Ireland that once ran through it.

By the mid eighteenth century, towards the end of the reign of King George II, Blackrock and Booterstown had become fashionable seaside resorts popular with the upper classes. At that point in their history they appeared to have it all – money, good looks, sea views

. . . then it all went **horribly wrong**. For reasons that have never been satisfactorily explained – lead in the water supply is one theory – the area suddenly embraced **revolutionary nationalism**. Almost overnight, Blackrock and Booterstown had more violent republicans than you'd find at a Wolfe Tones concert in Bray.

Lord Edward FitzGerald, who grew up in Frescati House, led the United Irishmen during the 1798 rebellion. **James Stephens**, from George's Avenue in Blackrock, founded the Fenians in around 1850, of which **Charles Kickham**, from Montpelier Place, was a leading member. **Eoin MacNeill**, from South Hill Avenue in Booterstown, was chief of staff of the Irish Volunteers during the 1916 Rising, while **Éamon de Valera**, who spent most of his life in Blackrock, once hid a revolver underneath the altar in the chapel in Blackrock College in his early days as a revolutionary. At one point the British considered closing all of its military prison camps in Ireland and erecting a **big fence** around Blackrock and Booterstown instead.

Sensitivity about the part their area played in severing ties with Britain might explain why the locals were happy to see so many buildings of historic interest turned into **shopping centres**, including FitzGerald's own Frescati House, of which he wrote in a letter to his mother: 'I am sitting in the bay window with all those pleasant feelings which the fine weather, the pretty place, the singing birds, the pretty wife and Frescati give me.' It's reassuring to know that some traditions survived the wrecking ball. Today, the place is still very much associated with **birds** and **pretty wives**.

Famous Residents

Count John McCormack, the famous tenor, lived on the Rock Road in Booterstown. His performance at the Eucharistic Congress in Dublin in 1932 was watched by a live audience of one million people and is remembered to this day as Ireland's first-ever super-concert, some seventy years before the first Oxegen music festival.

Brian O'Nolan, *aka* Flann O'Brien, *aka* Myles na gCopaleen, grew up in Blackrock, as did **Bob Geldof** and lots of violent nationalists the locals would prefer to think of as someone else's. **Sir William Orpen**, official war painter during the First World War, was born in Stillorgan. During his days as a draughtsman he also designed a housing estate, not – as his experience of the horrors of the Western Front might lead you to believe – in Bray or Coolock, but in Stillorgan itself.

Blackrock College 🍎

Everyone hates them and they don't care. And why would they? Ireland's very own Eton has been turning out brainy boys since the time of the Famine, and a huge number of Ireland's **high-achievers** in the arenas of finance, law, sport and the arts have passed through Williamstown's hallowed halls. If Rock boys come across as superior, it's simply because they are.

Among its famous alumni are **Éamon de Valera** and **John Charles McQuaid**, former Taoiseach and former Archbishop of Dublin respectively, who helped shape modern Ireland – or, rather, the Ireland that came *before* modern Ireland, which to be honest was **a bit of a shithole**.

Blackrock College is synonymous with rugby. The school has won the Leinster Schools Senior Cup an astonishing sixty-five times and has been contributing players to the Ireland team for as long as the game has been played. **Brian O'Driscoll**, **Fergus Slattery** and **Brendan Mullin** all learned to play rugby in the famous **baby-blue and white hoops** of 'Rock'.

The school is also proud of people like **Flann O'Brien**, **Liam O'Flaherty**, **Padraic Ó Conaire** and **Anthony Cronin**, who overcame the crippling

The famous gates of Blackrock College, South Dublin's very own Eton. Abandon the price of a decent-sized family car, all ye who enter.

handicap of not being very good at rugby to forge a living for themselves as writers.

The school was founded by a Frenchman, **Père Jules Leman**, a member of the Holy Ghost order who travelled to Ireland in 1859 to recruit missionaries for Africa. On his arrival, Leman was shocked to discover **a nation of thickos**, this being the days before expensive grind schools. He decided to set up an élite institute of education, and in 1860 the order acquired Castle Dawson and almost 60 acres of land between Blackrock and Booterstown for its school. It was originally known as The French College, though the style of schooling was more Anglocentric than anything else.

A WORD FROM ROSS

I'm not what you would call a reader, roysh, but it was actually JP who pointed out to me that bit in Bob Geldof's autobiography where he grabbed the old man's Beamer or whatever, drove up to Rock and did a load of u-eys and handbrake turns, basically ripping the shit out of the pitch.

So the first time I did sixth year, roysh, I had the idea of following in Geldof's, well, tyre tracks. I was egged on, it has to be said, by Fr Fehily, our principal, who gave me the keys to Brother Alphonsus's Volvo along with a warning that if I was caught, I was of course on my own and the school would have to, like, disown me and deny any prior knowledge of the operation, which was fair enough.

So this Thursday night, roysh, I hit Blackrock, pull off the Rock Road into the place and head straight for the main rugby pitch, which is where Drico and the boys would have been, like, training every day. So I drive onto the pitch and I'm about to do my first handbrake turn, roysh, smack in the middle, when all of a sudden, these goys appear from, like, nowhere, we're talking seven or eight of them, we're talking boarders and they just, like, surrounded the cor.

They're all giving it, 'Who is this goy?' and 'What's he doing here?' and of course I'm kacking it, roysh, thinking, I am SO focked if they call the Feds. So I decide to play it Kool and the Gang, roysh. I wind down the window and I go, 'Sorry, I'm lost. Must have taken, like, a wrong turn onto the pitch and shit?' And they're looking at me, roysh, going, Should we believe him? Then one of them turns around and he's like, 'What are you doing here anyway?' and suddenly I'm put on the spot, roysh, and I end up going, 'I'm, em, looking to buy a Christmas tree.' Well, they seemed happy enough with that until one of the goys copped that it was the first week in February and one of the others went, 'Hey, that's Ross O'Carroll-Kelly, the outhalf from Castlerock who's a seriously shit-hot rugby player and is SO going to play for Ireland one day,' and that's when all hell broke loose.

I've had wedgys courtesy of pretty much every school worth mentioning in the Leinster area, but I never had one like this. One of my stones didn't drop again until the second week in March.

Despite the **insane wealth** of most of the parents who send their sons there, the school has a proud record of carrying out **charitable works**. The sale of **Christmas trees** raises in the region of €100,000 for St Vincent de Paul every year. Included among the school's past pupils are the Legion of Mary founder Frank Duff and Bob Geldof, who, through Band Aid, Live Aid and Live 8, raised hundreds of millions of pounds towards famine relief in Africa. It's believed that if Geldof succeeds in his goal of ending world poverty, the school might even forgive him for saying on *The Late Late Show* that the place was a **dump** and for making shit of the rugby pitch by performing wheelspins on it in his old man's car – a stunt that made him an instant hero with anyone who ever went to Terenure College, Gonzaga, Clongowes, Belvedere College, St Michael's College, St Mary's College, CBC Monkstown, St Andrew's College, Pres Bray, CUS, Templeogue College . . .

Good Old Boys

It's often said that once you go to Blackrock College, you never really leave and it's true that most of the school's former students maintain a **lifelong allegiance** to their old *alma mater*. This is far from unusual in South Dublin. The past pupils of most of the area's élite, fee-paying secondary schools see themselves as part of an informal, fraternal organization bound together by shared interests, beliefs and values. 'Old boys', as they're known, always help each other out, in a manner similar to the **Freemasons**.

Below is the kind of conversation that might take place at a job interview involving an employer and interviewee, both of whom attended the same prestigious South Dublin secondary school:

Interviewee: Sorry I'm late. Just couldn't get my shit together today.
Employer: Well, you're here now . . .
Interviewee: Yeah, in body more than spirit, it has to be said. No, I had a serious amount to drink last night. I think I actually woke up still mullered.
Employer: Em, look, shall we start? I, em, see from your *curriculum vitae* that you've never worked in a bank before?
Interviewee: Correct.
Employer: In fact, you've never worked at all. Apart from one summer in – where was it? – Cape Cod. *Shelling prawns.*
Interviewee: Yeah, I was on a J1er. Actually, I put down there that I did it for three months. I only stuck it for, like, three weeks.
Employer: And you dropped out of college after one

year. Well, I say, *college*. Am I right in believing this was a *private* college?

Interviewee: You most certainly are. See, one of my biggest problems has always been getting up in the morning. Most of the lectures started before ten. It was like, fock that!

Employer: And I see you failed every subject in your Leaving Certificate?

Interviewee: Whoa, correction, Dude – not *every* one. There were actually two exams I didn't turn up to. No focking prizes for guessing why! Hey, I hope I'm not giving you the impression I've got a problem here.

Employer: Well, to be honest . . . Oh, wait a minute . . . Hey, I see here that you went to my old *alma mater*, Castlerock College!

Interviewee: Yeah.

Employer: Welcome to the firm.

Shopping ♀

Shopping – are you kidding? These people practically invented it. Nearby Stillorgan is the site of Ireland's first-ever shopping centre, which opened in 1966. Since then Blackrock and Booterstown have let nothing – not even history and architecture – get in the way of their desire to shop.

Blackrock has two shopping centres – the **Frascati**

Centre (on the site of the aforementioned flattened Frescati House) and **Blackrock Shopping Centre**. They are separated by the Blackrock Bypass, but pedestrian lights on this busy thoroughfare ensure that when Blackrock decides to shop, the traffic literally comes to a **halt**.

Blackrock has become a haven for fashionistas. The ladies here always look well and that's no surprise as there is no end of posh boutiques for them, including **Sandz** and **Monica Peters**.

For men, there are two looks that are always in fashion – rugby-*chic* and marine-casual. For the latter, there's **Nautica** in Blackrock Shopping Centre, where you can pick up your Helly Hansen jacket, Canterbury trousers, Dubarry Docksiders – in fact, all the clobber you'll need for having a drink in the sailing club bar. If it's the rugby look you're after, you're spoiled for choice, but check out **Diffney** in Blackrock Shopping Centre and the excellent **Gentlemen Please** on the Main Street, both of which will kit you out in the old rugger regalia so you won't feel out of place while you're here.

There's furniture aplenty, too, with a range of shops that reflects Blackrock's mania for Scandinavian and Spanish interior design. The section of the Main Street opposite the library has been nicknamed Baltic Drive, with shops like **Nordic Living** and **Danish Design Kitchens** fitting out local homes with Scandinavian hand-tufted rugs and free-standing, Narvic mirrors in Norwegian oak. Then there's **KA-International**, the Spanish Interiors Company whose aim is to 'democratize interior decoration'. Not even Blackrock, where marketing-speak is the second language, has a clue what that's all about, but it's well known that if you're after a *chaise longue* or a *banqueta estepa capitone* (that's a stool, to you), then this is the place to come to.

The **Millrose Gallery** and the **Waldock Gallery** have paintings by a wide range of artists, including many scenes of the coast around Blackrock, without which no South Dublin vestibule is truly complete.

A WORD FROM OISINN

Blackrock kids are known to be the most obnoxious little shits in the world. A huge number of them are called Lorcan, as well. Actually, here's a little tip for parents: call your kid Lorcan and he'll turn out a focking brat just as sure as he'll turn out bent if you call him Julian. There's no point in scratching your head later and wondering did you do something wrong.

Like I said, Blackrock has lots of little Lorcans who seem to have the run of the town on Saturday mornings. You're enjoying a latte, a stack of pancakes with maple syrup and Gerry Thornley's preview of the big match and there's one running around your table, making a noise like an Indian, working off his 7Up sugar rush, while his parents stare into space, oblivious to the irritation the little focker's causing. Of course, it's the most natural thing in the world for you to want to pick the thing up by the ankles and beat it like a focking rug.

Oh yeah, you'll hear the occasional, pleading 'Lorrr-can' from his old pair, but the kid's got the message long ago that his parents are too PC to belt him when he's bold.

It was a couple of years ago, after sticking out a sly foot and causing one Lorcan to snot himself in the middle of Café Java, that I came up with probably my first ever business idea – a child-slapping service, where mums and dads who don't believe in hitting their kids could bring them to me and I'd do it for them.

I had a price list and everything worked out. Three slaps across the back of the legs with an open hand was ten sheets. With a wooden spoon, it was fifteen. And it was twenty-five if you wanted me to take a leather strap to the kid's orse. I'd actually found premises in Blackrock and everything. Went to see the bank manager, but he wouldn't stump up the bread. Probably because he was Blackrock College and I'm Castlerock.

If I had to choose a ladies' fragrance that captures Blackrock and Booterstown in a bottle, it would probably be *Ghost Cherish*, which embodies purity with individuality for a woman with a strong sense of herself, a subtle sensuality and deep feelings, basically a woman who's a modern romantic – honest and open.

The Atomic Wedgy

A **wedgy** is a **practical joke** that involves gripping the victim's **underpants**, twisting them until they **snap**, then hanging them from a **tree** or other public place where they are visible to all and sundry. Designed to inflict pain *with* humiliation, this laudable trick was first performed by Randy Warne, a high-school student in Sacramento, California, in September 1973.

The increasingly popular, though far more dangerous, **atomic wedgy** involves the removal of the underpants *over* the victim's head. Harry Adams, a second-row on Blackrock College RFC's third team, is credited with being the first man to successfully perform the manoeuvre when he relieved full-back Simon Gannon of his boxer shorts after the team suffered a heavy defeat to Bective at Stradbrook Road in January 1997. A **statue** marks the spot.

Superquinn

It's difficult for the younger generation to grasp what life was like before Tesco colonized Ireland. There was a time when there were no twenty-four-hour warehouse-sized supermarkets selling everything from **organic leeks** to **48-inch plasma-screen televisions** right around the clock. Then, the weekly grocery shop was a chore. You pushed a trolley with a defective wheel up and down narrow aisles, and you chose from an even narrower range of products. There were only **two types of bread**, for example – brown or white. And, difficult as it is to believe, you couldn't buy pak choi or organic tofu for love nor money.

Except in Blackrock.

Superquinn was a splash of exciting colour in the drab, monochromatic pre-Tiger world. Even back in the bad old eighties, when Ireland was so poor it looked like it would be repossessed, it was somehow comforting to know that you could still get a reduced-salt batard and block of Wensleydale with apricots from Feargal Quinn's gleaming flagship store in Blackrock Shopping Centre.

Quinn is a master of innovation and was the first supermarket owner in Ireland to introduce **online shopping** and a **loyalty bonus scheme**. Along with Riverview and West Wood memberships and the platinum AmEx, the SuperClub card remains a staple in every South Dublin wallet.

Southsiders love being listened to – it's one of the reasons they talk so loudly – and part of what has made Superquinn such a success story is the way it responds to **customer demands**. It was the first supermarket to remove sweets from its checkout areas after receiving complaints about 'pester power'. And it introduced other parent-friendly initiatives, such as playhouses for children and assisted bag-packing. Hell, if it's raining, they'll even walk you to your car with a brolley over your head. It's not surprising that the weekly shop in Superquinn has become more a **social event** than a necessary household task. On Thursday evenings and Saturday mornings the aisles are full of mums and dads with strangled Southside accents, talking about golf and gardening and whether the Cotswold is more wonderful with or without onions and chives.

How to Get Around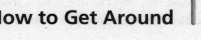

Centrally located, Blackrock is essentially the hub of South Dublin and **every vehicle in the Dublin Bus**

fleet passes through it – and Booterstown – at some point in its journey. The Dart also stops at **Booterstown** and at **Blackrock** stations.

Where to Stay ⌕

Key to accommodation:
Luxury ★★★
Seriously opulent ★★★★
Pretty much palatial ★★★★★

★★★★ Blackrock Clinic
What do you mean, there's nothing wrong with you? Get a boil lanced, your eyebrows plucked or your Henri-Lloyd sailing jacket surgically removed. *Anything*. If you can afford it, this **private clinic** is one of *the* places to stay in South Dublin. The coffin-dodger's mantra – 'I don't like hospitals' – is never heard here. Blackrock Clinic has all the ambience of a **hotel resort** in the Tropics – indoor palms, water cascades, rare birds and Ennio Morricone covers played on the pan pipes. There's no vomiting bug here. Nobody sleeps in the corridors, and trolleys are only used to wheel your **five course, *à la carte* dinner** to your bedside.

★★★★★ Radisson SAS St Helen's Hotel

They call this Dublin 4 – wouldn't we all if we could get away with it? No, this is *really* Booterstown, but spending a night at St Helen's is like scoring a British Royal and going back to her place.

Strolling around this spectacular, converted eighteenth-century mansion, you'll catch yourself speaking in an **awfully-awfully accent** and have to fight the urge to **shoot an animal** with a double-barrel shotgun. The only double-barrels here, though, are on the guest list.

This is a seriously swanky pile of bricks that is five-star all the way. Built in 1750 for Thomas Cooley, MP, the house has been beautifully restored and contains over 150 luxury rooms and suites, two excellent restaurants, a conservatory bar, a state-of-the-art gym and a snooker room. The price? If you have to ask, you don't belong here. Kindly leave. Or make do with afternoon tea in the marble Ballroom Lounge, or the best **buffet breakfast** in town in the Talavera restaurant.

If you *can* afford it, ask for a suite with a balcony and a view of Dublin Bay, order up a bottle of Châteauneuf-du-Pape and remind yourself what a wonderful thing it is to be **seriously loaded**.

Where to Eat

Talavera in the Radisson SAS St Helen's is without doubt the best Italian restaurant in Dublin. Head chef Giancarlo Anselmi is a kitchen Da Vinci, producing authentic dishes from Tuscany and Basilicata, which are served up in a number of candle-lit dining rooms with cosy fireplaces. If you have a penchant for risotto with asparagus and truffle scent, it's probably God's way of telling you that you have too much money.

At weekends the locals flock to the Radisson for the famous Sunday lunch at **LePanto**, before a stroll around the hotel's famous gardens and a couple of straighteners in the bar.

Dali's on the Main Street in Blackrock has been called the Southside Unicorn, its excellent grub making it a favourite for middle-earning barristers and RTÉ types.

There's an **Eddie Rocket's** on the Main Street in Blackrock and another in nearby Stillorgan, where the clientele are the privileged teens who'll grow up to run the world – or at least the world as you know it. Enjoy watching them knock back hillocks of nachos with guacamole and vanilla malts today, because tomorrow you might be facing them across the counter of the bank, begging them not to repossess your home.

TGI Fridays on Newtownpark Avenue in Blackrock
is a demonstration of the awesome spending power of
South Dublin's twenty-somethings, who can pay twenty
quid for a burger and chips without cribbing about it
for a week.

Entertainment

Twice a year the caravans arrive in Booterstown in
their dozens and park in a field along the seafront –
and the locals don't even call the Gardaí! That's
because these caravans belong not to members of the
Travelling community but to one of two **circuses** that
have become synonymous with Booterstown. Duffy's
Circus, which arrives in June or July every year, and
Fossett's, which arrives in October, have been
entertaining children for generations, though obviously
not too many local children, what with circuses being
considered terribly working class in this area and
parents fearful that their children might pick up
headlice or, worse, **'howiya' accents**.

Blackrock is just 7 km from Dublin City Centre and
yet you could literally grow a beard in the time it takes
to drive from one to the other in the morning and
evening rush hours. So bad is the traffic congestion on
the coastal route known as the **Rock Road** that many
people now make the commute into the city at 3.00 or

4.00 am, catching three or four hours' sleep in the
company car park before beginning work. Then they
wait until 10.00 or 11.00 pm to drive home. Like the
crush of commuters on the Tokyo underground, it's
well worth seeing the chaos on the Rock Road. In
particular, look out for the way the traffic is reduced to
a single lane just north of Booterstown, while cars in
the right-hand lane queue for up to a mile to cross the
busy commuter railway line through an old-style **gate-
crossing**, which is closed on average every three
minutes. Marvel, too, at the world-famous **Blackrock
Bypass**, which features an amazing six sets of traffic
lights in the space of 300 yards. Watch the traffic drive
through Blackrock village to 'bypass the bypass'.

Travelling through Booterstown on a public bus, you
might well hear a voice shout, 'Phwoar, look at the tits
on that.' It's quite likely the voice will be referring to
the beautifully colourful songbirds that have made their

home on **Booterstown Marsh**. South Dublin's only concession to bogland is home not only to common birds but to some of the world's most endangered migratory species, including Black-tailed Godwits. It stinks.

A WORD FROM CHRISTIAN

I remember when I was a kid, Mum and Dad used to take me to the circus, sometimes Duffy's, sometimes Fossett's, and even though they were both pretty good, I'd always be there thinking how cool it would be if, like, Circus Horrificus came to Booterstown? As in the alien freak show that used to, like, travel from star system to star system? Actually, Jabba the Hutt recruited Malakili – as in the main rancor keeper – from Circus Horrificus. He's supposed to be running a restaurant in Mos Eisley now . . .

Pubs and Clubs

Blackrock is rightly renowned as the best place in South Dublin to go on a pub crawl.

Sheehan's is a cool, sophisticated pub, all polished floors and dark-wood furnishings, and tends to attract the after-work crowd. If you fancy the arse off the bird in the bank, the chances are you'll find her here on a Friday night.

Across the road **Tonic**, with its whitewashed walls, mirrors and spotlighting, has a wine-bar ambience. There're some fine works of art to see in here – not just the paintings that cover the walls but the girls with pouts like blow-up dolls who stare through you as they pass by. If you decide to chat one up, don't bother telling her she's beautiful – she already knows.

The Mad Hatter has had its fair share of growing pains, but, like Lewis Carroll's wacky hatmaker, you can't but have a soft spot for the place. In 2003 'The Hosh', as it's affectionately known, introduced all-you-can-drink nights (€40 for goys; €25 for birds) and got slated by the government, who accused them of setting targets for binge-drinkers. At the time of writing, the Hosh is closed but is set for another rebirth soon.

For rugby there's **Gleeson's** in Booterstown. It's an interesting pub and has several alcoves to which they've given names – rooms, they call them. With its blood-red walls and framed paintings of old hunts, it has the feel of a private members' club and is owned by the uncles of Keith Gleeson, the Ireland rugby international. If you don't have a ticket for Lansdowne, this is the next best seat from which to watch the game. Although if you're from South Dublin, you'll probably have one anyway.

The Wicked Wolf is the pub that puts the rock into Blackrock. Long and narrow, with high tables and benches arranged around the walls like a railway station waiting room, once night falls it suddenly kicks off like a box of firecrackers in an old folks' home. It earned its 'rep' in the 1990s as a place you could go to take off your shirt and play air guitar on the bar to 'Sweet Home Alabama'. The pub has changed hands since then – for almost €4 million in 2000. The Lynyrd Skynyrd CD came with it.

The Playwright on Newtownpark Avenue is a great 'battle cruiser' that's often mistaken for a soccer pub because of its association with former Ireland manager Mick McCarthy. The only Celtic jersey ever seen in this big, spacious pub is the one belonging to the former joint-owner, which once hung in a frame behind the bar. The people who drink here are Blackrock pure-breeds.

The Orangerie is a Victorian-style conservatory bar in the Radisson SAS St Helen's Hotel that attracts South Dublin's new royalty: barristers and builders – these builders being the ones with manicured fingernails who wouldn't know which end of a trowel to hold. The name is believed to be a nod towards the local fashion for sunbed tanning.

Suggested Itinerary in Blackrock & Booterstown

Pint in the Avoca. Pint in Jack O'Rourke's. Pint in the Wicked Wolf. Pint and a short in the Breffni. Pint and a short in the Mad Hatter. Pint and a short in Sheehan's. Pint and a cocktail in Tonic. Get refused by the Playwright. Sleep in a bus shelter.

The high diving board at the old Victorian swimming baths is a reminder of darker days, when Blackrock witnessed poverty, verrucas and fat women in bathing costumes that looked like cheese wires.

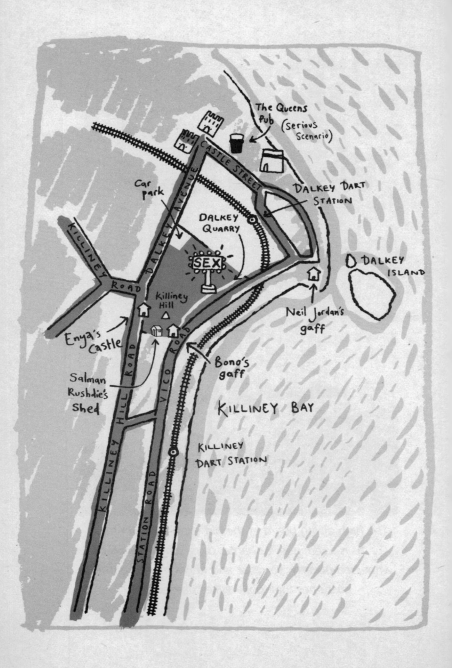

6. Killiney & Dalkey

Welcome to Bel-Éire! The *crème de la brulée* of the legal, business, music and movie worlds have been buying up this little coastal corner of South Dublin since the mid 1990s. In fact, there is no better metaphor for the Celtic Tiger era than the spectacle of tribunal-rich lawyers and dot.com millionaires engaged in a battle royal with the stars of stage and screen for the **Mock-Gothic mansions** with the best views of the sea . . .

Sorrento Terrace, the most sought-after address in Ireland. If you fancy being Neil Jordan's neighbour, you better have money. They look down on oil barons in this part of the world.

Killiney and Dalkey lie on an elevated plane some 100 metres above sea level, and people in the surrounding environs look up and dream of one day living there. And it's little wonder. This is, quite simply, the **most beautiful place on Earth**.

Killiney Hill Park, with its stunning views of Dublin Bay, Bray Head and the Sugar Loaf, was opened in 1887 to honour Queen Victoria's fifty years on the throne, though the older, more settled residents here see themselves not so much as West Brits than as West Neapolitans. Killiney Bay was once famously likened to the **Bay of Naples**. Though no one can actually

One of Dalkey's few remaining working-class families get ready to leave, after selling their two-bedroom kennel to a chinless IT millionaire for a record 2.8m euros in 2006.

remember who said it, the locals completely lost the run of themselves and began renaming all the roads in the area in a distinctively Italian vein – Sorrento, Monte Alverno, San Elmo, Vico and Capri.

Killiney has little or no village to speak of, though Dalkey more than makes up for it with its **world-famous pubs**, **gourmet restaurants** and shops selling everything from bespoke bedrooms to bespoke kitchens. Near by, Dalkey Island and Bulloch and Coliemore harbours are just two of the other reasons why houses in the area are so sought-after. Today, 1930s council-built slum dwellings that look like sets from *Angela's Ashes* are changing hands for upwards of €1.5 million.

Killiney and Dalkey are home to a huge population of privileged teens, high-fiving rugby jocks and some of the thinnest girls alive **outside of the Third World**.

History

There is some disputed evidence of an ancient Celtic civilization in the area. Close to the ruined church on Marino Avenue in Killiney lies what many believe to be a genuine **Druid's Chair**, though a number of historians have said it's as fake as the area's Mock-Gothic and Mock-Tudor houses that are changing hands for small fortunes.

In 1831 a stone coffin containing a perfectly preserved skeleton was dug up in a field called Quatre Bras, near Killiney. Also in the coffin was a small fortune in ancient Saxon and Danish coins, suggesting that even in the ninth and tenth centuries the people in this part of the city were **rolling in it**. The name 'Killiney' is in fact derived from the Gaelic *Cill* (village), *Ineíon* (indecently) and *Leínín* (loaded).

Dalkey is a Norman town. Its main street is dominated by the Goat and Archbold's castles, where English and French traders stored their wares from the fourteenth to the sixteenth centuries to protect them from the pillaging O'Byrnes and O'Tooles – the forebears of today's **skangers**. The same tradition is maintained to this day. Dalkey and Killiney people are forced to fortify their homes with reinforced steel windows and alarms to stop the latter-day O'Byrnes and O'Tooles from travelling out on the Dart to burgle them blind.

In 1742, after a bout of severe frost, local philanthropist John Mapas offered to make money available for the relief of the poor. He insisted they **work for their money**, however, and commissioned what stands today as one of South Dublin's most famous landmarks – the obelisk atop Killiney Hill. Mapas's efforts to alleviate desperate poverty by getting people to build something absolutely pointless for a few bob is regarded as Ireland's first ever **FÁS course**.

Towards the end of the sixteenth century, the main shipping port in South Dublin was moved from Dalkey to Ringsend, and the area experienced a slump, from which it took almost three centuries to recover. Extensive quarrying for rock to build Dún Laoghaire

Harbour, as well as the arrival of the railway in 1843, marked the start of a period of prosperity for Dalkey, which economists predict **will never end**. Wealthy home-buyers and property investors have bought up most of the poor people's homes, and it is estimated that by 2010 working-class people will have been completely eradicated from Dalkey.

South Dublin's Hollywood Hills

All Northsiders, naturally, want to live on the Southside. Tragically for them, the vast majority never will. However, some Northsiders who have done well out of life have managed to escape the horrors of North Dublin for a better life on the other side of the city.

Bono, the lead singer with U2, grew up in Ballymun, but bought a mansion on the slopes of Killiney Hill once he hit the big time. When he paid what now seems a ridiculously modest one million punts for his Vico Road pile in 1990, he became the first resident of South Dublin's very own **Hollywood Hills.**

Within ten years some of the biggest names in showbusiness were stumping up eight-figure fortunes for their very own **turreted mansion** overlooking the bay. Nowadays, whenever a house changes hands at a private auction, there's wild speculation about who the newest resident will be. **Jack Nicholson**, **Michael**

Douglas and **Brad Pitt** all have coveted homes in the area. **Van Morrison**, rock's crankiest man, lives here, as does **The Edge.** Every day, hundreds of busloads of tourists visit this once sedate, leafy paradise to snatch a glimpse of a famous celebrity, or just to see how the rich and famous live.

Quite a number of musical relics of the 1980s have washed up here, including **Lisa Stansfield**, **Jim Kerr**, **Joe Elliott** and **Chris de Burgh**.

Movie director **Jim Sheridan** owns a pad on Coliemore Road in Dalkey, while **Neil Jordan** loved his house on Sorrento Terrace so much that he bought a

Ayesha Castle, a turreted, six-bedroom pile on Victoria Road, is the home of Enya, who popularized elevator music and who remains the most recognizable symbol of Ireland . . . in northern Japan.

second one. And at €7 million a go, who could blame him?

In the late 1990s Killiney became *the* place to live for racing-car drivers. **Damon Hill**, **David Coulthard** and **Eddie Irvine** all bought pads there. Irvine remains something of a role model to the area's well-heeled youth, having bedded a succession of stunning women and spent most of his twenties driving a Ferrari round and round in circles, which is what many of Killiney and Dalkey's twenty-somethings spend their summer Sunday afternoons doing.

A WORD FROM JP

I sold a few houses in this area when I was working for my old man. Never sold one in Killifornia – as we used to call Killiney Hill – but I admit I used to dream about being asked to, then retiring on the commission. I was like everyone else in those days – all about money. I did quite a few things I can't say I'm proud of. When Enya paid IR£2.5 million for her place, well, suddenly Killiney was *the* place to live, and pretty soon we were flogging poky little semis there for a million squids. Of course, not everyone could afford one. That's when I came up with the idea of referring to Ballybrack as 'South Killiney' in our sales bumf.

Nowadays, I realize that this kind of behaviour is wrong. A home shouldn't be regarded as an index of one's social status – it is a shelter from life's turbulent seas, given by God.

I like this passage from the Bible: 'Is it time for you yourselves to be living in your panelled houses, while this house remains a ruin?' This is Haggai 1:4 I'm quoting, one of the prophetic books of the Old Testament, written about 520 years BC, though I think its lessons remain especially relevant in these consumerist times.

'Now this is what the Lord Almighty says: "Give careful thought to your ways. You have planted much but have harvested little. You eat, but never have enough. You drink but never have your fill. You put on clothes but are not warm. You earn wages only to put them in a purse with holes in it." This is what the Lord Almighty says: "Give careful thought to your ways. Go up into the mountains and bring down timber and build the house, so that I may take pleasure in it and be honoured."'

AND JUST TO SHOW HOW SERIOUSLY PEOPLE TAKE THE PROPERTY BUSINESS IN THESE PARTS, A WORD FROM FIONN

Dalkey was the main point through which bubonic plague – or the Black Death – entered Ireland in the middle of the fourteenth century. The disease was caused by the bacterium *Pasteurella pestis*, which was carried by fleas hitching a ride on the backs of rats. It's estimated that between 1348 and 1350 it wiped out one quarter of the entire population of Europe. To this day, the people of Dalkey refuse to speak about the role their town played in one of the worst epidemics mankind has ever known – for fear it would affect local property prices.

Knacker *Chic*

At some point in their mid to late teens, many boys and girls from Killiney and Dalkey start to effect the behaviour, accent and manners of Dublin's poorer social classes. Most begin speaking with hard, inner-city accents and using coarse language, eventually graduating to shoplifting and accusing strangers of staring at them, or other imagined slights, as a pretext for beating the shit out of them. According to psychologists, Knacker *Chic*, as it's known, is a simple act of teenage rebellion in which adolescent boys and girls reject their privileged backgrounds and the values of their wealthy parents, often out of feelings of guilt. It's a temporary condition, which usually lasts until they discover just how much money can be made from **commercial law** or **futures**.

Shopping 🍦

Killiney village consists of little more than a shop and a pub, though Dalkey is heaven for anyone with a bit of room on their Visa card. The twenty-something solicitors and stockbrokers who have been buying up the village's local authority-built shanties are **nesting** – renovating their new homes and filling them with trendy modern furniture and expensive art.

Dalkey has a number of galleries, including the **Tramyard Gallery** and the **James Gallery**, where you can buy wonderful works of art by contemporary Irish artists. As they say in this part of the world, they're **the new wallpaper**.

It's estimated that each of us spends one third of our lives in bed – or twice that if your parents are wealthy and you grew up in Killiney or Dalkey. Suffice to say

Like Paris, London and New York, Dalkey is justifiably proud of its cultural quarter, which is situated between Dalkey Credit Union and Clegg's Shoe Repairs.

that the bedroom is the most important room in your life. **The Bedroom Studio** will provide you with one that you'll never be ashamed to bring a 'bird' back to. Check out the Jensen Supreme Vital with its adjustable massage function, which stimulates blood circulation, relaxing your legs, back, shoulders and neck and providing superior sleeping comfort. You could ride Zara Phillips in that and never feel like you were punching above your weight.

Meanwhile, the **Design House** will provide you with a cooking and dining area so state-of-the-art that your maid won't want to go home in the evenings. In this little corner of the world you're no one unless you have a handmade kitchen in natural timber with an American-style, two-door fridge and elevated coffee bar.

How to Get There

Dalkey is serviced by the **7D, 8, 46N** and **59**. It's also on the **Dart** line, and Dalkey station is right in the middle of the village. Killiney is notoriously difficult to access – the reason they built it on a hill in the first place. The **59** bus is rumoured to go there, but, as they say in these parts, 'You'll be waishing.'

The Dart does stop at Killiney, but from the station it's a thirty-minute hike uphill to the little village, and the **altitude sickness** usually claims those intrepid souls who attempt it.

Your best bet is to bring your car. Except there's no parking.

Where to Stay

Fitzpatrick's Castle Hotel in Killiney is an eighteenth-century castle set in rolling parkland on the brow of Killiney Hill, overlooking the bay. Its 113 bedrooms are decorated in traditional style, with warm, dusk tones and dark-wood furnishings, each with Internet access, cable television, a CD player and a games console. They've got a great restaurant (**PJ's**), an elegant bar (**The Library**) and a chauffeur who'll pick you up at the airport. The castle's former dungeon was once the site of a famous nightclub (**Jesters**). Many South Dublin men still make pilgrimages there, revisiting the spot where they got their first **'bit of tit'**.

A WORD FROM CHRISTIAN
Jesters is now, like, the Dungeon Bar. Lauren likes it, but I'm not a fan myself, probably because the word 'dungeon' makes me think of the pit underneath Jabba the Hutt's desert palace on, like, Tatooine? I know a lot of people did, but I never felt sorry for the rancor when Luke killed it, although apparently on the planet Dathomir they've actually, like, domesticated these creatures? They're supposed to use them as, like, pack animals and even personal mounts, but I don't know if that's true . . .

Where to Eat

There's an old saying that in Killiney and Dalkey, there's only one eight o'clock in the day. As home to Ireland's biggest population of people who don't have to get up early in the morning, it's no surprise that in these parts brunch is the favourite meal of the day – or the only meal of the week in the case of the area's emaciated female population.

Dalkey's wonderful **In** starts dishing it up at ten o'clock every morning and by midday is still serving goat's cheese crostinis and calamari and lychee salads to hungover Trustifarians. Around the corner there's the wonderful **Nosh**, whose buttermilk pancakes with toasted banana and maple syrup are the only reason many Dalkey and Killiney folk are vertical before one o'clock in the afternoon. And that's not to forget **Idlewild**, which serves the best cappuccino in all of South Dublin to the backing track of local ladies fighting with each other over the privilege of who's going to pay.

The Main Street in Dalkey has so many good Indian, Thai and Chinese restaurants (**Jaipur**, **Tiger Becs**, **Kingsland**), it's been nicknamed **Dalkasia.** And if you're the type who knows his turbot from his halibut, the chances are you'll already know about the **Guinea Pig**, the seafood restaurant of which Dalkey people are smugly proud. They've been serving food out of 17 Railway Road since 1957, when **John Wayne**, **Maureen O'Hara**, **John Ford** and **Peter Ustinov** used to go there to be fed and watered. If you think Bono, Liam Neeson and Cliff Richard have been piling on the

A WORD FROM ROSS

I suppose you could say I'm pretty well known in this port of the world, having had more than my fair share of success with the birds here. There's, like, three schools for girls out that direction – we're talking Holy Child Killiney (Collars Up, Knickers Down), we're talking Loreto Dalkey (Virgins on the Rocks or Whores on the Shore, depending on how lucky you get) and St Joseph of Cluny (the Rich Teas). I know for a fact, roysh, that back in the day the teachers in all those schools used to hand out photographs of me, warning birds to basically stay away from me. It was like, 'He might be very good-looking, have an unbelievable bod, be an incredible rugby player, have loads of chorm, blah blah blah – but basically you'll end up getting hurt. That's as sure as your dad's going to buy you a cor for your eighteenth.'

Did the warnings work? They did not. I did so much damage out there the Red Cross had to set up a focking shelter to deal with the broken-horted.

pounds lately, it might be because they can't stay away from the place. Dublin prawns. Galway mussels. Wicklow lamb. That's not to forget the **Dalkey crab** –

which is that you have to switch off your mobile phone in the restaurant, preventing the local daddies from telling their friends about how their son has just made the Senior Cup team, **at the top of their voices**.

Most Dalkey people would tell you they'd probably starve to death were it not for **Select Stores**, the old-style grocery store that stocks Yogi tea, aubergine pickle, dried kaffir lime leaves and all the other basic necessities.

Ententainment

Fitzpatrick's Castle Hotel has a **leisure centre** with a fully equipped gym, 22-m pool, on-deck jetted spa, Scandinavian wood sauna and steam room. Young mums gather in the beauty salon every morning to enjoy aromatherapy and reflexology and talk about how little Conor or Emily said their first word the other day and it was 'focaccia'.

Killiney Golf Club on Ballinclea Road is a nine-hole parkland course that features some of the most spectacular scenic views anywhere in Ireland. It's often unfairly characterized as a club for middle-aged 'yaws' and old farts. Killiney welcomes visitors, of all things, on Mondays, Wednesdays and Fridays. Admittedly, though, its nine holes make it the ideal South Dublin course for Alzheimer's sufferers.

The **car park at Dalkey Hill** is the most popular venue for having sex outdoors in South Dublin. Make sure to get there early, though. By 11.00 pm it's usually full of teenage boys fumbling with bra straps in their mothers' Fiat Puntos.

Killiney Beach is the most beautiful stretch of coastline in South Dublin, though bathers should beware: the water might look inviting, but fifteen minutes in there and you're unlikely to see your testicles again for a fortnight.

Yogalates is the craze that's sweeping Killiney and Dalkey like . . . well, like the plague of 1348. It's an internationally popular form of exercise that blends the best of the ancient Yogic spiritual discipline with the skeletal exercise dynamics of Pilates. There are literally hundreds of classes available in the area. Each session

finishes with the chanting of the Sanskrit word
Namaste, which means, 'The Divine in me recognizes
the Divine in you'. Interestingly, divine happens to be
Killiney and Dalkey's most popular word, and you will
hear it used to describe everything from a walnut-and-
chrome table lamp to a walnut-and-mango muffin.

Pubs and Clubs

Dalkey is known to have the most vibrant, seven-day-
a-week pub scene south of the city, with most of its
young people never having done a decent day's work
in their lives. The rivalry between the various
establishments is intense, resulting in recent years in
a battle to out-renovate each other. Many innocent
trees have been lost in the process.

Finnegan's serves arguably the best pint of Guinness
in the village, but is regarded as a pub for the older
crowd; in Dalkey that means anyone over the age of
twenty-five. When you've started getting to Finnegan's
early to get a seat, you know you've reached a
watershed in your life – it's time to accept that job
offer from the old man.

It took a long time for the people of Dalkey to refer
to the pub that was formerly called The Arches by its
new name, The Mariner and Bailey's. Many people
thought the red neon **In** was there for the benefit of

those who were too pissed to find the front door. Nowadays, In has become one of South Dublin's most popular haunts to have a drink and ogle emaciated beauties with sink-plunger pouts, mid-distance stares and cheekbones you could hang your sailing jacket on.

Around the corner from **In** there's **The Club**, a great pub full of lively young people – and Feds. People travel from miles around to watch rugby matches on its famous big screen. The satellite dish is also capable of picking up 'soccer', though, this being Dalkey, there's not always a call for it. Beautifully renovated in recent years, the pub features a painting of the Dalkey coast that covers three sides of the ceiling – the village's very own Sistine Chapel.

There's no praise too lavish for **The Queens**, the former Irish Pub of the Year and hangout for the biggest rides in Dalkey since 1745. And that doesn't mean a quarter to six. Securing a seat in the beer garden out front on a sunny summer's day is a reminder of what a wonderful thing it is to be alive and loaded. Sit over a bowl of mussels and a pint of Guinness and watch the procession of beautiful people pass by.

Ivory used to be McDonagh's – The Queens' snot-faced younger cousin – but it's recently been given the famous wine-bar make-over. Pop in now on a summer's afternoon and you'll find people eating sushi and watching Wimbledon on the biggest screen in Ireland.

A WORD FROM OISINN

A last word about the birds in Killiney and Dalkey. There's unbelievable rivalry between the girls in Holy Child Killiney and Loreto Dalkey as to which is the 'coolest school'. This competition extends to hockey, debating, musicals and whose girls manage to score the most players on the Leinster Senior Cup-winning team.

But the biggest bone of contention between the two schools is who invented the craze of saying, 'Oh my God!' very loudly at the start of every sentence. Holy Child Killiney claim they started it, but Loreto Dalkey insist it's theirs.

If you were to ask me to choose a ladies' fragrance that captures the very essence of Killiney and Dalkey, I'd probably go for *Euphoria* by Calvin Klein, a creamy, lush fragrance that smells of summer and sugar almonds.

Suggested Itinerary in Killiney & Dalkey

Get up, like the rest of Killiney and Dalkey, at 10.00 am. Enjoy a brunch of goat's cheese crostini in In, then attend a real-life property auction, watching some 25-year-old computer nerd battle it out with a wizened old rock star for an imitation castle overlooking the bay. Climb Killiney Hill and enjoy the view. Notice how peaceful even Bray looks from up there. Join a group of Spanish students on a tour of the homes – or at least the remote-controlled gates – of the rich and famous.

Enjoy a lunch of pan-seared lamb's liver with crispy bacon, onion and mustard jus on creamed mash in the Queens, while 'scoping' some of Europe's most beautiful women. Enjoy nine holes of golf at Killiney Golf Club, followed by dinner in the Guinea Pig. Try the St Brendan's deep-fried Brie followed by the Bradan Deilginnis, along with a nice bottle of wine. Trip across to Finnegan's for a nightcap. Chat-up an authentic Dalkey honey, dropping into the conversation the fact that you've just bought the turreted mansion you saw auctioned for €10 million this morning. Suggest a late-night skinny dip on Killiney beach. Go for treatment for exposure and gangrene at nearby St Columcille's Hospital.

*Dalkey people were forced to build castles to
defend their property from nearby Sallynoggin,
in the years before Eircom Phonewatch.*

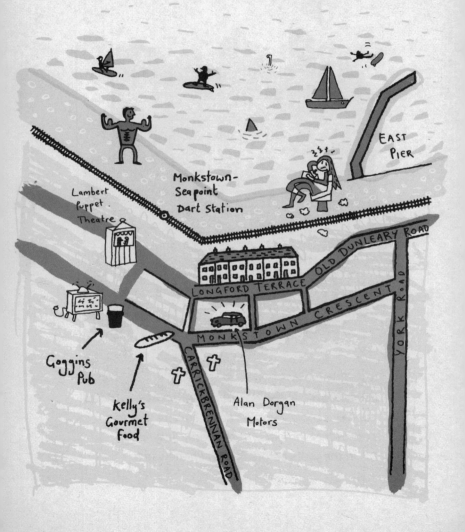

EAST PIER

Lambert
Puppet
Theatre

Monkstown-
Seapoint
Dart Station

OLD DUNLEARY ROAD

LONGFORD TERRACE

MONKSTOWN CRESCENT

YORK ROAD

Goggins
Pub

Kelly's
Gourmet
Food

CARRICKBRENNAN ROAD

Alan Dorgan
Motors

7. Monkstown

Wedged between Blackrock and Dún Laoghaire on the South Dublin coast, Monkstown is where **Bohemia** meets **Pacifica**. It's a great big hunk of Greenwich Village, topped with a dollop of the Californian coast (served, naturally, with fennel bread and a rocket, apricot and pine-nut salad) . . .

Monkstown – pronounced mink stain – is a vibrant clash of cultures, home to more **surfing jocks** than Huntington Beach, lots of very posh people, and a coterie of famously sullen painters and writers. Most of the wealth that does exist in these parts is passed down through the generations. Women here love to '**gorden**', and the hedges and lawns are much like the local accents – well clipped.

Monkstown's artists are among the most anguished in the world and it's often said that if you put them in **Abu Ghraib** for a week, they wouldn't be any more tortured than they already are. Thousands of tourists flock to this little corner of South Dublin every year just to eavesdrop on them as they discuss the inner torments of the artist's soul, such as how to squeeze complicated concepts into the restrictive rhyming patterns and syllabic scheme of a Petrarchan sonnet, or how to squeeze through a rear first-floor bathroom window when the landlord calls looking for the rent.

Monkstown mummies and daddies tend to send their children to exclusive schools to learn **Gaelic**, an ancient, mumbo-jumbo language that's of use to absolutely no one once they leave school. When you're inheriting the old man's business, though, it's an indulgence you can well afford.

Like most of the teenage girls who live here, Monkstown is shrinking at an alarming rate and is now no more than one square mile in area. Yet it remains

Local artists Dave and Tom make the keynote speech at the opening of the Monkstown Arts Festival in January 2007. Since 2004, the Revenue Commissioners have accepted cans of Dutch Gold as a legitimate business expense for the area's artists.

known the world over for the restaurants on the famous **Crescent**, its **fine houses** from many periods and the puppet theatre that – careful here – seduced Michael Jackson. The rubber-faced King of Pop once enjoyed a private performance at the famous **Lambert Puppet Theatre**, which featured characters from the 1970s children's show *Wanderly Wagon*. Jackson later admitted sharing a bed with **Foxy Loxy** and **Padraig the Horse,** but denied plying **Mr Crow** with alcohol and touching him inappropriately.

Monkstown beach is one of the most beautiful in the world, its white sand and turquoise sea providing a sharp contrast to the beaches on the Northside, which are all white bodies and pink toilet paper. And Bob Marley music. None of that here. Monkstown is where young men with **blond highlights** and **Action Man chests** ride the swells or show off their skills on a windsurfer, while managing to keep their Ray-Bans propped on top of their peroxide-perfect heads.

History

For centuries Monkstown was a rural area of mostly pastureland and was in the possession of St Mary's Abbey until the Reformation, when, much like the Church, it underwent its own schism. Half of Monkstown decided they wanted to become **toffs**, while the other half – that bit referred to today as Monkstown Farm – decided they'd sooner stay the way they were.

Monkstown has always known on which side its organic multi-seed bread was low-fat buttered. During the United Irishmen's rebellion of 1798, most residents of Monkstown went before a judge to swear **loyalty to the Crown**.

There then followed 200 years in which the town became stupidly rich.

A WORD FROM FIONN

Monkstown Castle is well worth a visit, even though there's only a small portion of the original structure still standing. It was built in the thirteenth century by the monks of St Mary's Abbey, from whom the name of the village is derived. The castle passed through various hands down through the years. After the failed rebellion of 1641, the then incumbent, Walter Cheevers, was deported to Connacht, and Oliver Cromwell eventually granted the castle to General Edmund Ludlow, who had played a key role in the defeat of Charles I in the English Civil War.

Which is interesting . . .

Famous Residents

Monkstown has always been a beacon for arty types, and some of Ireland's most creative – and terminally lazy – people have chosen to make it their home. Go for a drink or a walk along the seafront and chances are you'll be accosted by a man in an Aran sweater with smelly hair, selling a booklet of his poetry.

Not all of Monkstown's artists struggle to make the rent, though. **The Edge** from popular Irish group U2

lived in the town for years, and **Sinéad O'Connor** –
high priestess of Rastafarianism and whatever you're
having yourself – now calls it home.

Shopping ♀

Monkstown has everything for the shopper – provided
you're looking for **surfboards**, **fast cars** and
expensive claret. The Crescent, the village's main
drag, has no butchers but has *two* speciality shops for
watersports enthusiasts – **Wind and Wave** and
Windmill Leisure. Equipped with a wide range of gear
by Helly Hansen, Henri-Lloyd, Lowe Alpine, Canterbury
and Dubarry, for generations these two shops have
been kitting out UCD students in a style Monkstown
pioneered – marine casual.

And for those who *do* intend coming within an arse's
roar of the sea, these shops stock everything from
surfboards to bodyboards, and from windsurfers to
wakeboards, and even buoyancy aids – though
obviously not of the type you get offered in **spam
email**.

At last – world-class Tokaji! A cheeky little number
with a cute nose and a great body. You too can talk
about wine **like you want to ride it** in either of the
village's two specialist wine merchants: **Searsons** or
Eno Wines. Don't go wandering in there looking for

Albanian Riesling at four bottles for a fiver, though. They don't *do* central-heating for the homeless. These people know their oats – except they'd probably call them oaty overtones, perhaps with subtle brambly notes.

Why not buy a flashy car? **Alan Dorgan Motors** is where Monkstown's daddies go to sell their two- and three-year-old BMW 3 Series 318 Ci autos and perhaps pick up a **Mercedes 350 SL** – the old Monkstown Runaround – for the wife.

A WORD FROM OISINN

I don't know when it was that CBC Monkstown last won the Senior Cup, but I know the Beatles were still mates at the time. In fairness to them, though, those goys always give you a seriously hord game – and they never give up. Although sometimes they should. I remember we kicked their orses one year and as we're coming off the pitch, one of their goys, Prionsias MacStiofáin – big into their Irish names for whatever reason – he turns around to me and goes, 'Well, at least we're still in the All-Ireland Debating Championships.' I think Ross spoke for us all when he weighed in with his famous comment, 'Yeah, roysh!'

How to Get Around

Monkstown is reachable by road, rail and sea. The port of Dún Laoghaire is near by, connecting Ireland to Britain in just over three hours by conventional ferry and in just 100 minutes by Stena Sealink's **high-speed catamaran**. Allow yourself another 100 minutes to drive the couple of hundred yards through the traffic-choked seafront road to Monkstown.

There are two **Dart** stations near by – one at **Monkstown and Seapoint**, the other at **Salthill**.

The Nos **7, 7A** and **8** serve the village from Dublin City Centre. The **46A** also passes through Monkstown during a long and circuitous journey that also takes in Ayers Rock, Angkor Wat and the Puerto Moreno Glacier. It's the only Dublin Bus service on which meals and drinks are served and a **full duty-free service** is offered.

Kite Surfing

Kite surfing is the new craze among Monkstown's beach bums. You strap yourself onto a small surfboard or wakeboard and use the windpower from a large, controllable kite to pull you across the surface of water

In the most recent census, 27 per cent of Monkstown's 18- to 25-year-old males listed kite-surfing as their full-time occupation, while 32 per cent listed it as their religion.

– at speeds of up to **70 kmph**. The challenge is to control both at the same time – to steer the board on the water while piloting the kite in the sky. On any given day you'll see hundreds of young men in Monkstown, spending upwards of eight hours a day practising their jumps, tricks and turns in anticipation of it one day becoming an Olympic sport.

Enough Surfish to Get By

Surfers – or surfer dudes – have their own language, which will probably sound foreign to your ears. Here are a few key phrases you'll need to 'catch the drift' on the beach in Monkstown:

Accessory man: A surfer who has everything – except an ability to surf.
I am, like, SO amped: I'm very charged up.
Hang ten: Hello.
That's off the Richter, Dude: That's great.
Banzai: A shout given by surfers as they shoot the curl.
Beach bunnies: Good-looking girls who hang out at the beach.
I would *hate* to be that good: I would love to be that good.
Ankle busters: Small waves.
I just caught a serious ride: I just rode a big wave.
That was bitching: That was top class.
Dude, you are hot-dogging: You're showing off.
Rad: Excellent.
Big gun: A 9-ft surfboard, designed for big waves.
He's ripping it up: He's performing very well on his surfboard.
That's awesome: That's good.

Dude, you're the zenith: You're the best.
Dudette: A female surfer.
That guy is extreme: That guy is crazy.

A WORD FROM ROSS

It's pretty well known that I can't swim, roysh, although I have been known to strut my abs and pecs up and down the beach, giving birds everywhere a major thrill. I have to admit, roysh, that there's some pretty stiff competition down on Monkstown beach. Those surfer dudes, most of them look like johnnies stuffed with conkers. You'd want to go on a six-month course of anabolic steroids just to avoid feelings of inadequacy.

Where to Eat

Monkstown Crescent is South Dublin's very own restaurant district, with every imaginable food available – except fast, naturally. There are no burger bars here. Instead, there's **Waldo's,** an Italian restaurant currently satisfying South Dublin's mania for pappardelle, and **FXB** for those who want honest-to-jaysus Offaly beef and chips.

Running your spoon through the seafood chowder in **Wrights Brasserie** is like drag-netting in a fish farm – it's stuffed full of the stuff. **Valparaiso** specializes in Mediterranean cooking, and their crayfish paella always has the locals dreaming of Marbella, or wherever their Continental investment property is located.

A visit to Monkstown would not be complete without a slow browse through the shelves in **Kelly's** gourmet food shop. This is where Monkstown goes on a Saturday morning for its pasta and Parmesan bread sticks, chestnut spread, wine-flavoured jelly and olives the size of horses' testicles.

The Monkstown Mumble

Monkstown men are so wealthy that somewhere around middle age they reach the point where they can't be bothered to speak in full sentences any more. This has given rise to a form of patois known as the Monkstown Mumble, the main feature of which is a low, unintelligible muttering sound, out of which a single, recognizable word will suddenly appear, typically a noun intended as a command. A Monkstown man might turn to his wife – or a servant – and say, 'Rrrrrrrr . . . Mnnnnn . . . Arrrrrrr . . . FIRE,' which means, 'I'm cold – light the fire.' Or you might overhear him in a shop saying, 'Vrrrrrrr . . . Mnnnnn . . . Wwwwrrrrr . . .

Paper,' which translates as, 'Give me an *Irish Times*, please.'

Entertainment

'If everybody had an ocean,' the Beach Boys sang in their famous paean to the surf-and-sun lifestyle of West Coast America's youth. Monkstown is all of Brian Wilson's most extravagant dreams come true. Sun, sea, sand and sailboarding – and not just sailboarding but windsurfing, canoeing, power-kiting, kayaking and, of course, surfing. Monkstown has **uncrowded reefs and beach breaks** with predominant offshores galore, as well as waves that hold up to 30 ft.

Goggins is one of the best-known pubs in South Dublin. If you want to watch an Ireland rugby international but don't want to see grown men playing drunken games that involve pulling down their trousers, then this is a great alternative to Blackrock.

Suggested Itinerary in Monkstown

Enjoy a pot of Cubita Molida Ground and a late breakfast of organic crackers with fennel and caraway seeds and *terrine de Chevreuil aux Cèpes* in Kelly's. Walk the seafront between Monkstown and Seapoint. Watch a local artist draw the twin chimneys of the ESB power station or – better still – wait until eleven o'clock on Wednesday morning and watch a whole load of them draw the dole at Cumberland Street in Dún Laoghaire. After a pub lunch in Goggins, suck in your stomach and make your way down to the beach to learn how to windsurf or ride a 20-ft breaker. Go to Alan Dorgan Motors and splash out a few Ks on a Mini Cooper for your daughter's eighteenth birthday. Realize you're suffering from sunstroke.

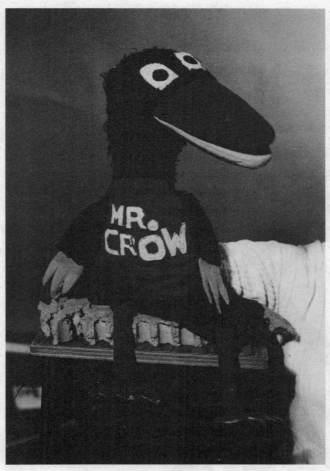

Mr Crow was among the stars of Lambert Puppet Theatre who entertained Michael Jackson in Monkstown. Crow has strenuously denied ever using skin fader.

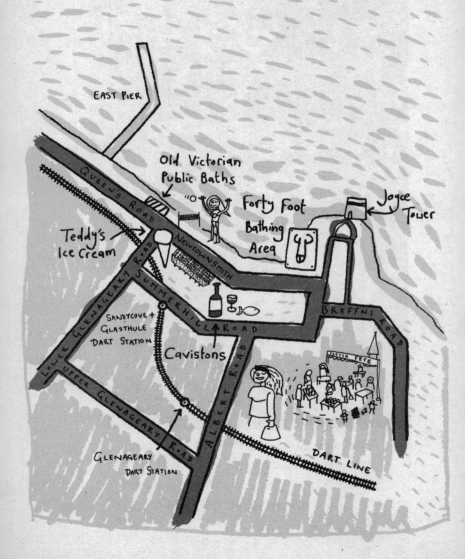

8. Sandycove & Glenageary

It's often said that to live in Sandycove is to be singled out for God's special blessing. It's no surprise that so many **giants of popular entertainment** have been besotted by the place, including Britney Spears, Tom Cruise, Party Boy from 'Jackass' and James Joyce, who used it for the opening scene of his gibberish classic *Ulysses* . . .

Sandycove is Pleasantville-on-Sea, a picture-perfect utopia where even dog shit on the pavements doesn't smell. Glenageary is its landlocked soulmate, home to a huge number of South Dublin's **old-money rich** and **West Brit Protestant gentry**, a fact reflected in the hundreds of houses in the area named *Ben Nevis* and *Sandhurst*. Both villages are located between Dún Laoghaire and Dalkey, and whether your pleasure is walking, dining or simply playing fast and loose with your **credit card limit**, they will seduce you with their snotty, upper-class charm.

There's a lot more to Sandycove and Glenageary than tennis clubs, Victorian terraces and streets with ridiculous names like Wilmont Avenue and Otranto Place. Here you can get up in the morning and do almost anything – enjoy a jojoba soak sensation, send your dog for a mint-and-lavender scrub or smoke a Cohiba the size of a baby's arm. And you can take out your mickey! The Forty Foot bathing area is famous for its nudist swimmers. It's where South Dublin men do something literally that they also enjoy doing figuratively – showing people the size of their balls.

If publicly exposing yourself without fear of prosecution is not your bag, there are a hundred other activities that will appeal to all tastes. You can shop in **posh boutiques**, buy **fine wines** that cost 300 quid a bottle and eat rich **caviar** until it brings you out in hives.

This little paradise is sure to enchant you, just as it has the stars of stage and screen. **Jane Seymour** loves shopping here, as do **Mrs Bono** and **Rosanna Davison**, a bad girl who in 2003 was voted the biggest ride in the entire world. **Tom Cruise** and **Nicole Kidman** spent a lot of time in Sandycove during the filming of *Far and Away*, which may explain why their accents in the film were like no Irish accents anyone had ever heard before.

Martin Sheen was once spotted walking the

SANDYCOVE OR GLASTHULE?

In Northern Ireland the use of either 'Derry' or 'Londonderry' is a cipher by which the user identifies with one or other side of the community. So it is with Sandycove and Glasthule – two nominally different areas with no discernible boundary between them.

If you refer to the area as Glasthule, it's generally assumed that you are working class.

While most people know that Sandycove is one of the most desirable addresses in Dublin, this quirky sub-group of people is proud to say that they are from Glasthule. Until, that is, they're selling their houses, when they suddenly live in Sandycove.

seafront area and **Britney Spears'** visit to posh frock shop Rococo has become an urban legend. The singer is said to have followed up her spree in Sandycove by taking the Dart to Bray – to get a tattoo.

It goes without saying that there are **no tattoo parlours** in Sandycove or Glenageary.

History

Napoleon Bonaparte loved his decadence – antiques, paintings, fine food and even his own type of brandy. He would have loved Sandycove and Glenageary – and didn't the people there know it, erecting a 40-foot-high tower with a 24-pounder cannon in the roof to persuade him to keep his filthy foreign hands off their *œufs de lompe* and VSOP. The Martello Tower in Sandycove succeeded in keeping Napoleon out, but not the **French influence**, which is reflected in the fact that Sandycove consumes more *foie gras per capita* than, well, France.

Today, the inhabitants of Sandycove remain as protective of their little paradise as their forebears were. In the 1990s plans were mooted to develop the nearby Victorian swimming baths into a **water-leisure centre** and the green area on the seafront into a car park. The locals considered the horrors that this would visit upon the area – verrucas, Speedo 'posing pouches', Daihatsu

A WORD FROM ROSS

Yeah, they're no strangers to my handsome mug out that direction either. There's a big boarding school out there for birds called Rathdown. A lot of goys call it Betdown, though I've always thought that was way horsh. There's always a few little nuggets of gold in there, roysh, even if you do have to pan through a lot of muck to find them.

In 1999 I did what many people considered the impossible, attending the debs balls of Rathdown and Mount Anville on the same night, without either of my two dates for the evening suspecting a thing.

I took a bird called Siún Freehill to the Rathdown debs in Jurys in Ballsbridge and Carla Queenie to the Mount Anville one in the Berkeley Court around the corner. I spent the evening pegging it between the two hotels. I bought two boxes of Butler's chocolates, went to two gaffs for pre-debs drinks, even ate two focking chicken supreme dinners. Heroic is the word you'd have used to describe it.

Of course, the word got around town. Everybody was talking about it. So I ended up being officially banned from attending the Rathdown debs for life for – get this – 'emotional cruelty'. What can I say? There's a lot of birds out there – and only one of me to go round.

Charades – and gave the developers something like Napoleon would have got, a bombardment with a fusillade of **petitions** and **solicitors' letters** until the plan capsized and sank without trace.

Sandycove and Glenageary have a proud history of dissent. Evidence of the role the area played in the **women's liberation movement** can still be seen today in the famous MEN ONLY sign in the Forty Foot bathing area, under which someone has painted a polite: NO, WOMEN, TOO. Note the perfect punctuation. Even in the fervour of the burn-your-bra sixties, **correct grammar** was still considered more important than gender emancipation.

Famous Residents

Oliver St John Gogarty moved into the Martello Tower in Sandycove in 1904. Gogarty was a physician and ear surgeon who gave it all up to become a Dublin wit, at a time when the market was flooded with them. Gogarty, who counted W B Yeats among his fans, won a bronze medal at the Olympics in 1924 – for poetry. This was back in the days when Ireland won medals and didn't have to give them back a few weeks later.

Gogarty took **James Joyce** in as a flatmate, but quickly fell out with the famous freeloader who

elevated twaddle to an art form. Joyce spent only seven days in Gogarty's 'gaff' (above), complaining that the rent was exorbitant. 'It's focking Sandycove!' Gogarty is reputed to have told him. '*Hello?*'

Roger Casement, poet, patriot and troublemaker, was born in Sandycove in 1864. His work in the British consular service in the Congo, where he denounced the forced labour system, won him few admirers in this part of the world, however. Nor did his activities in the lead-up to the Rising in 1916, when he tried to enlist German support in the Irish rebellion. Had he had his way, Marine Parade would be called Kaiser Wilhelm Walk, Teddy's Ice Cream parlour would be selling *bratwurst* and Britney Spears would be shopping not for dresses but *lederhosen*.

Another notorious troublemaker, singer **Sinéad O'Connor**, grew up in Glenageary, though locals will tell you that she was 'more towards the Sallynoggin end of things'.

Shopping

If you have a hankering for posh frocks, antiques or fine food and wines, you'll find everything your heart desires in Sandycove or Glenageary. Glasthule Road is the area's very own Rodeo Drive. Pop into **Rococo**, **Denise** or **Mrs E** and you're sure to need a Sherpa to get your bags back to your car.

Mitchell & Son Wine Merchants is where you'll find reasonably priced wines – as well as reassuringly pricey ones. The back of the shop is where you go if you're looking for a bottle of Château Ducru-Beaucaillou St-Julien for €166, or a nice Château Angélus 1995 for €199. Hang around long enough and you'll hear customers saying such things as, 'It's flinty and sharp, yet with a certain unctuosity, not to mention big chewy tannins,' and other hilarious poppycock worthy of Joyce himself. Mitchell's also stocks a wide range of Cuban cigars, including Romeo y Juliettas and Partagases the size of the dog turds that litter the seafront area in summer.

At **Buckley's** auction house you can pick up

anything from a William IV extending dining table to a
George III longcase clock – for the price of a modest-
sized house.

A WORD FROM OISINN
Being in the beauty business myself,
I know how much birds love pampering
themselves. And a serious amount of
them end up in Bliss, which is owned by that Clare
McKeon, who I seriously would, if you're asking.
It's all eyelash tints, argan facial massages and
jasmine blossom floats. That's Sandycove for you.

If you asked me to choose a scent that captures
the essential essence of Sandycove, it would have
to be *Touch of Pink* by Lacoste – an expression of
magnetic and carefree sensuality, like a shoulder
freckled by the sun.

Cavistons

You know the feeling. You've just settled in for the
night when you discover you're clean out of *terrine de
faisan aux noisettes* and gluten-free shortbread. What
do you do? Well, if you've been favoured by God with a
home in Sandycove or Glenageary, you can nip around
to **Cavistons**.

This famous gourmet food emporium is an institution
on this part of the Southside and is a **hive of activity**
at any given time of the day, whether it's tennis moms

popping in for a French stick and some Mediterranean-style cheese and beetroot blush, or Southside dads sniffing out the finest Caspian traditional *œufs de lompe* or some terrine of pheasant with boysenberries to wow the partners at tonight's 'dinner porty'.

Cavistons draws not only gastronomes and connoisseurs of fine food but also those who like to **people-watch**. You could kill a couple of hours

A WORD FROM JP

Like a lot of people, I associate Sandycove with Cavistons on Christmas Eve. My dad would go there some time around mid morning to collect the turkey, goose or occasionally mallard, and, of course, the spiced beef, chestnut and sausage-meat stuffings, mince pies with lattice crusts and brandy butter. Until quite recently I would have regarded this as being a happy childhood reminiscence. Now all I can think about is the unnecessary extravagance of it and, of course, the waste of food.

Proverbs 23 tells us: 'When you sit and dine with a ruler, note well what is before you, and put a knife to your throat if you are given to gluttony. Do not crave his delicacies, for that food is deceptive.'

standing in this compact little shop, watching the locals being 'posh' – men in golf sweaters with clogged-up arteries being knowledgeable about Gouda; women with **cut-glass accents** saying 'divine' and 'fab-a-luss' a lot, with accompanying limp-wristed hand gestures.

Then there's the food. Caviar. Yams. Fresh wild salmon. Venison. Blueberries. Truffles. *Foie gras*. You'll feel like you've broken into the pantry at Buckingham House. And don't miss the famous cheese counter – which stocks **every type of cheese known to man**, except, of course, those plastic-coated processed slices that are very popular with poor people.

How to Get Around

Sandycove and Glenageary are both well served by public transport, which is unfortunate. The Dart and bus services have made this once unspoilt paradise all too accessible for working-class people – and the Gardaí are powerless to do anything about it.

The No. **8** bus serves – for want of a better word – Glenageary Road. The **111** also passes through Glenageary, as do the **7** and the **45A**.

Happily, Sandycove is not so well served. The **59** is a bizarre and thankfully little-used bus route that takes in the Sandycove Road. There's also the **7D**, which stops in Sandycove, too, though mercifully only once a day.

There are Dart stations at **Sandycove & Glasthule** and at **Glenageary** – accounting for the number of working-class people you'll see on summer days walking through the town wearing soccer jerseys, especially those of the popular team Glasgow Celtic.

Where to Eat

How many times have you heard it said that you simply can't get good roast guinea fowl in Dublin any more? Well, **Odells** is the best possible retort to that. In the 1990s Hollywood celebrity couple Tom Cruise and Nicole Kidman ate there. Nicole absolutely loved the flake. In fact, she married him. As for the food, they loved that too, both licking their plates clean. Chris de Burgh is a regular as well, though don't let that put you off. He doesn't sing.

There could be no better recommendation for **Daniel's** than to say that Patrick Guilbaud has eaten there more than once, as have Jean Kennedy Smith, Liam Ó Maonlai and Pat Kenny. Chef and host Daniel Harkin can perform miracles with a saucepan and a bit of halibut, but it's the Lobster Thermidor and ten-hour seafood chowder that'll bring you back time and time again. They also serve an indigenous working-class dish called 'goujons of plaice', known locally as the Glasthule Lobster.

A WORD FROM ROSS

You can't go to Sandycove, roysh, without checking out Teddy's, the famous ice-cream place on the seafront? It's a great place to go for a first date. The beauty of it is, roysh, if you end up copping off with a bird in, say, the Club of Love or, like, Reynords and can't remember what she looks like, you can arrange to meet her – we're talking midweek – for a Teddy's and a walk on the pier. If she turns out to be a hound, the night's only cost you the price of a 99 – or two, if you pay for hers as well. Plus, meeting her outside Teddy's allows you to check her out from a discreet distance, so if she turns out to be seriously horrendous, you can get the fock out of there, no questions asked.

If it's lunch you're after, take the Lexus for a spin down to **Cavistons Seafood Restaurant**, one of the slickest little restaurants in town, where the chef is so skilled that even the cod in curry sauce tastes sophisticated.

If prawn and basil salad with gazpacho sauce is your thing, then you could do a lot worse than **Tribes**. The things these people can do with simple, standard ingredients, like ham hock risotto and *osso bucco* with lemon foam, make the mind boggle. Whether it's a cannon of pork, a shoulder of lamb or a gaggle of geese, you'll be so excited, you'll be chewing the menu before you've even ordered.

Entertainment

Every July, Sandycove and Glenageary have their own version of the marching season – the **Parish Fête Season**. While their Ulster cousins are dressing up in sashes and bowler hats to remind Catholics of the result in 1690, the Protestants in this quiet corner of the world have their own show of strength – organizing tray bakes and marrow-growing competitions (below) and selling old junk from their attics to each other.

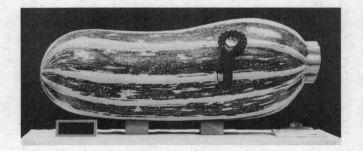

Bloomsday is also celebrated with great gusto, with devotees of Joyce's famous book of nonsense dressing up as characters from it and mincing around at the

Martello Tower, which is the setting for the first scene of *Ulysses*. Since 1962 the tower has operated as the Joyce Museum, containing his death mask, letters, first and rare editions of his books, as well as unpaid bills and final notices from the gas, electricity and phone companies that he didn't take with him when he left in a hurry.

The **Forty Foot Christmas Swim** takes place on the morning of 25 December each year, when locals celebrate the birth of the Son of God and saviour of mankind by jumping into the Irish Sea. Volunteers hand out flasks of whiskey, and there are competitions for the silliest bathing costume and the most fingers and toes lost to frostbite.

A WORD FROM CHRISTIAN

I always, like, crack up laughing when I think about Sandycove because I always call the people who come from there Sand People, as in, like, Sand People? I suppose what's even funnier about that is that I call the real Sand People, Tusken Raiders, which is, like, the proper name for them. They're, like, total nutters those things. I mean they actually hunt, like, krayt dragons, which is just, like, whoa! One of them hits you a belt with his gaffi stick and you'd know all about it . . .

Pubs and Clubs

Fitzgerald's was always *the* pub for hip twenty-somethings with money. In fact, it was often said that people went to The Eagle House to drink and to Fitzgerald's to be seen. But in 2005 that all changed when The Eagle House got an oak and smoked-glass make-over, 'out-Café-en-Seineing' its nearby rival and making a pitch for the local tennis and hockey club euro. The pub also underwent a fiendishly clever name change, with the unnecessary and time-consuming 'The' dropped and an 's' added, to become **Eagles House**. It's appropriate, too, as this is where, on a Friday or Saturday night, you'll find many of Sandycove's young eagles – beautiful, powerful, majestic animals, with their eye always on the main chance. A response from Fitzgerald's is awaited.

Suggested Itinerary in Sandycove & Glenageary

Get out of bed ridiculously early and take an invigorating plunge into the icy waters of the Forty Foot. Shake off the hypothermia with a mug of cappuccino in a local coffee shop and read some pages from *Ulysses*, especially the zany opening scene set just a couple of hundred yards from where you are sitting.

Visit Cavistons and pick up a fresh poppy-seed loaf, a wedge of Pecorino with black pepper, a jar of Mostarda d'Uva and perhaps some pure acacia honey with cut comb, and enjoy brunch on the spectacular seafront. Visit the Joyce Tower and become engaged in a conversation with a fellow Joycean about your love for the gobbledygook bestseller. Enjoy a late lunch in Cavistons Seafood Restaurant, making sure to try the tian of crab and grilled swordfish. Spend the afternoon shopping – either 'doing a Britney' by visiting Rococo and the other posh boutiques on Glasthule Road, or picking up fine wines in Mitchell & Son's, or furniture in Eminence. Then kick back for an hour or two. Enjoy a gin and tonic in the newly refurbished Eagles House and maybe some more laughs from Joyce.

Still hungry? Good, it's dinnertime. Don't leave Sandycove without enjoying the Lobster Thermidor with chopped onion and mustard cream sauce in Daniel's, or the roast guinea fowl with spiced apples in Odells. Then it's back to Eagles House or Fitzgerald's, or even The Deerhunter in nearby Sallynoggin, for a nightcap. Have one too many and get involved in an argument with a fellow customer who doesn't care that you think James Joyce is the greatest genius in the history of letters. Say some things you later regret.

Visit the A&E of St Michael's Hospital to have your copy of his mumbo-jumbo masterpiece removed from your arse.

Trips
Further
Afield

West Cork

You've been to D4 – why not visit C4? The city of Cork has a number of suburbs that have modelled themselves on Ballsbridge, most notably Montenotte, which in fact is sometimes called I Can't Believe It's Not South Dublin.

Like Dublin, Cork has its own privileged yachting class, who are known as the Merchant Princes. It's no surprise that their Dublin cousins have adopted towns like Kinsale and Baltimore as their favourite holiday destinations within Ireland.

Kinsale, which means 'Dalkey of the South', is just thirty minutes' drive south of Cork City and is famous for its gourmet restaurants, art galleries and leisure activities, which include golf, yachting and 'angling', which is like fishing, but for middle-class people.

Baltimore offers similar delights, though it should be pointed out that it's made up mostly of holiday homes and can therefore, on a winter's afternoon, resemble a North Dublin housing estate when there's a TV licence inspector on the knock.

South Dublin is the first language of Kinsale, Baltimore and a substantial part of Cork City.

North and West Dublin

The more intrepid visitor might like to venture beyond the cosy confines of the Southside and visit North or West Dublin to witness at first-hand the poverty, gun crime and high infant mortality rate that have made this part of the world infamous. The Northside has many attractions, including the Millennium Spire, the Abbey, Gate and Ambassador theatres, the Garden of Remembrance, the Four Courts, the GPO and the Customs House, as well as the Point Depot and Croke Park. The Westside has The Square Shopping Centre in Tallaght.

It must be pointed out that there are **significant dangers** involved in visiting these areas. However, by exercising a little caution, you can enjoy all they have to offer without experiencing anything more troublesome than having to hand over the contents of your handbag to a man wielding a **blood-filled syringe**.

A few words of warning

Do not carry your passport or large amounts of cash with you. Do not walk anywhere alone. Do not use the buses or the Dart at night. Avoid making unnecessary journeys after dark. In fact, don't go outside at all unless it's necessary.

A WORD FROM CHRISTIAN

If I had to go to, like, I don't know, Tallaght or somewhere like that, I'd love to do it in an All Terrain Scout Transport. You're talking 8.6 m high with a seriously heavy-duty cannon. It'd be like, 'Okay, just try to take the hubcaps off this baby.' Actually, out there, the fockers probably would try and tip it.

I suppose if you were going to go somewhere like the Square, you'd want an AT-AT walker, which takes no prisoners.

Under no circumstances should you attempt to use an **ATM** at any time. Most North- and Westsiders, while outwardly friendly, would cut your head off if they thought your fillings were gold. Keep mobile phones, BlackBerries and iPods out of view – make no mistake about it, these people will steal them.

Avoid wearing loud or ostentatious jewellery, as the locals will think you're **taking the piss out of them**. Only carry a handbag or shoulder bag that can be held securely. Do not attempt to carry a handbag if you are a man – you will likely be **kicked unconscious** by an angry mob.

Drivers should be alert when coming to a halt at traffic lights or a Stop sign. Keep the doors of your car locked at all times. When visiting the North City Centre area, park your vehicle in a controlled car park. If you must park on a residential street, you'll almost certainly be asked for money by a local youth wearing a fluorescent bib. The best advice is to pay him what he wants and try to think of being shaken down by this low-level protection racket as part of the overall experience.

There is, of course, the **danger of kidnapping**. Make sure that the areas you intend visiting are safe by asking hotel staff or the Gardaí for advice. Always let someone know where you are going.

The Garda Síochána do not yet have the power to shoot **beggars** in this part of the city, though visitors are asked not to give them money, as it only encourages this unwholesome activity.

Remember, North and West Dublin are currently in the grip of a gun feud between rival criminal gangs. If you plan to spend more than a couple of hours in either of these areas, it's worth investing in a **flak jacket**. These are widely available on the Northside and come in three styles: traditional combat black, Adidas and Burberry.

Remember, too, that the air in North and West Dublin contains more **pollutants** than it does on the Southside. This means that occurrences of light-headedness, breathlessness and mild headaches are not unusual. Drink a lot of water, but make sure it

has been purified first. If in doubt, use bottled water.

If you intend spending a lot of time exploring either region – perhaps visiting Tallaght, which in 2006 was twinned with the Palestinian town of Ramallah – you'd be advised to do so only in an **armoured personnel carrier**. These are fun, safe and available to rent in a number of different models. Splash out – literally – on the new, redesigned Chinese Type 63A, the only dedicated modern amphibious tank in the world, or go for the more meat-and-two-veg option of the DOZOR-B, which will provide protection against everything from small-arms fire to weapons of mass destruction.

ThesauRoss 🍎

A

Abs-and-pecs-olutely: *adv.* absolutely.

Accumulator: *noun* a run of good form in which one manages to 'cop off' with three or more girls in one social group.

Ace: *verb* to perform a function with minimum effort.

Airbags: *noun* a woman's breasts.
See also: Funbags; Lung capacity; Rack; Top tens; Walters.

AJH: *abbr.* a woman of low social status, from *Ah Jaysus Howiya* [a popular greeting in the socially disadvantaged areas of Dublin].

Alan Whickers: *noun, rhym.* knickers, e.g. 'Why are you getting your Alan Whickers in a twist?' [Alan Whicker (b. 2 August 1925) is a British journalist and broadcaster.]

Allied Irish: *noun, rhym.* an act of self-debasement popularly believed to induce blindness: Allied Irish Bank.

Anoraksia: *noun* a personality disorder characterized by an obsession with statistics and trivia.

Anto: *noun* a member of the poorer social class, so called because of the popularity of the name in Dublin's areas of disadvantage.

Apollo Creed: *noun, verb* the act of being intimate with an aesthetically displeasing stranger for one night only [in the movie *Rocky* (1976), world heavyweight boxing champion Apollo Creed offered a random nobody a shot at the title]. Example: 'Oh my God, what the fock is that? It's got Conor!' 'It's some total randomer he pulled. He said at the stort of the night he was going to do an Apollo Creed.' 'She's got a face like a chihuahua shitting a peach stone.' 'I know.' *See also:* Shot at the title.

Aristotle: *noun, rhym.* 1. courage, 2. a glass receptacle. Bottle. [Aristotle (384–322 BC) was a Greek philosopher, pupil of Plato and teacher of Alexander the Great, who established the methods of Western philosophy.]

Arms swinging, arrive with one's: *verb* to go to a house party without bringing any alcohol.

Atomic wedgy: *noun* an act of mild torture, usually practised by schoolboys and adult rugby players, in which the victim's underpants are twisted until they

snap, then removed from his body over his head; *verb*
to perform an atomic wedgy.
See also: Wedgy.

Ayrton: *noun, rhym.* a tenner, 10, from Ayrton Senna.
[Ayrton Senna (21 March 1960–1 May 1994) was a
Brazilian racing-car driver who won the Formula One
World Championship three times and died in a crash at
Imola in 1994.]

B

Babealicious: *adj.* (of a woman), aesthetically pleasing
to the senses and the mind.

Baghdad: *adj., rhym.* Mentally unstable; mad.

Bag it up: *verb* (of one's penis) to put on a condom.
Example: 'Bag that thing up before you point it at me.'
'Fock! I wouldn't have asked you back here if I'd known
you weren't on the Jack and Jill.'

Bail in: *verb* to initiate the process of sexual
intercourse, often after a long stand-off. Example: 'I
couldn't sit through another of her stories about how
she'd been hurt in the past, so I knocked back my drink
and bailed in.'

Ballistic: *adj.* extremely angry; *verb* go ballistic: to fly
into a rage.

Bally-go-on-go-on-go-on: *noun* a popular brand of mineral water: Ballygowan. [From the catchphrase 'Go on, go on, go on . . . ' used by Mrs Doyle in the popular TV series *Father Ted* (1995–8).]

Ballyjames: *adj.* up the Ballyjames (of a woman): having a child developing in the uterus [Brit., Aus. *informal,* Up the duff]: Ballyjamesduff.
See also: Damien, up the.

Batter: *informal* on the batter: to enjoy a long period of drinking alcohol, especially pints of lager – often prefaced by 'major', 'total' or 'serious'.

Battle cruiser: *noun, rhym.* a public house: boozer.

Battle formation, in: *adj.* (of a penis) erect.

Beamer: *noun* a BMW car.

Beaten with the ugly stick: *noun* ugly.

Beer goggles: *noun* the alcohol-induced distortion of vision that makes unattractive women look attractive. Example: 'I swear to fock, she looked like Liz Hurley last night. When I threw her out this morning she looked more like Red Hurley. I had the old beer goggles on, of course.'

Bee stings: *noun* small breasts.

Bells: *adv.* used to specify the hour in telling the time. Example: 'Dude, what time is it?' 'It's, like, seven bells.' 'Whoah, nice Rolex.' 'Whatever.'

Benny: *noun* 1. a man who has a sexual preference for people of his own sex: bent; 2. a term of abuse used randomly by adolescent boys.

Bet-down: *adj.* ugly. Example: 'Whoa! Jonathan's new bird is seriously bet-down.' 'Is there any proof that she's even a girl?'

Betty Ford: *noun* someone who spoils the fun for everyone by not drinking alcohol and by telling everyone in the pub that he/she is not drinking alcohol.

Be with: *verb* 1. to kiss; 2. to engage in sexual activity with.

Biddy: *noun* an elderly woman who is particularly annoying or interfering.

Big-match temperament: *noun* (of a man) the ability to withstand pressure situations, usually in relation to chatting up women.

Bladdered: *adj.* very drunk. Example: 'Dude, there's a focking traffic cone in my bed.' 'I'm not surprised, you were totally bladdered last night.' 'Hang on – no, it's not a traffic cone.'

Blankers-Koen: *noun* attractive girls, from Fanny. [Fanny Blankers-Koen (*née* Francina Elsje Koen) was an athlete from the Netherlands who won four gold medals at the 1948 Olympics in London, in the hurdles (200m, 100m and 80m) and the sprint relay (4 x 100 m).]

Blanket welding: *noun* the act of masturbating.

Blob strop: *noun* a condition experienced by women before or during menstruation, involving moodiness, irritability and swings of emotion. Example: 'I mean, she's crying. Just because I forgot her birthday.' 'Sounds like a major case of blob strop to me.' 'Let's get bladdered.' 'Cool.'

Blocks, up on the: the condition of menstruating. Example: 'Did you get your bit?' 'No, she was up on the blocks.' 'I hope you left there and then?' 'I did.' *See also:* Communists; Munster are playing at home; Painters; Period costume drama.

Blow chunks: *verb* to eject matter, often alcohol and fast food, from the stomach through the mouth; to vomit. Blowing chunks.

Boat race: *noun, rhym.* face

BOBFOC: *noun, abbr.* a woman with an attractive body but a repulsive face: Body Off *Baywatch*, Face Off *Crimewatch*.

Bod: *noun, abbr.* 1. body; 2. Brian O'Driscoll [the captain of the Ireland rugby team].

Bogball: *noun* Gaelic football.

Bogger: *noun* an unsophisticated person from the countryside or anywhere outside Dublin. Example: 'Look at those Munster fans. You have to give it to them – they are, like, SO the best supporters in the world.' 'Yeah. Focking boggers!'

Bogland: *noun* The countryside. Anywhere outside Dublin.

Bone: *verb* (of a man) to have sexual intercourse with a woman. Throw a bone.

Book: *adj.* cool. [If you try to type the word 'cool' in predictive text, you'll get the word 'book'.]

Borf: *verb* to vomit; *noun* matter vomited from the stomach: barf.

Borney: *noun* an argument, often between a man and woman: barney.

Bould thing: *noun* sexual activity, especially intercourse; *verb* do the bould thing. Example: 'Look at that Golf GTI across there in the cor pork. It's going up and down like a Northsider's knickers.' 'They must be doing the bould thing.' 'I'll say this, they've good suspension, those GTIs.' 'That's actually true.'

Brad Pitts: *noun, rhym.* a woman's breasts: tits.

Brayjing: *noun* a nickname for Bray, a town in north County Wicklow with a large immigrant Chinese population.

Brayruit: *noun* a nickname for Bray, a town in north County Wicklow with a reputation for lawlessness.

Bricking: *adj.* scared. Bricking it.

Britneys: *noun, rhym.* beers: Britney Spears. [Britney Spears (b. 2 December 1981) is a pop singer with four hit albums, sixteen singles, a Grammy and five MTV Europe music awards to her credit.] Example: 'Are you coming out for a few Britneys?' 'Yeah – and the rest!'

Brown bread: *adj., rhym.* dead.

Bualadh: /*boola*/*noun* bus, from *bualadh bos* (Gaelic, meaning 'applause').

Bucket of smashed crabs, a face like a: *noun* (of a woman) very ugly.

Bullet: *verb* take a bullet, to engage in an act of sexual intimacy with an unattractive woman so your friend can have her better-looking companion. Example: 'Look at her! She's SO like Tiffani Thiessen, you'd swear it was actually her. Oh no, look at her mate – she's a focking hog.' 'Dude, I'll take a bullet for you.' 'Okay, let's go.'

'Hang on, I'm just going to see can I get a glass of milk at the bor. Settle my stomach.'

Bullet in the chamber, a: *noun* a backlog of semen that can make a man appear desperate in a nightclub situation. Example: 'No, I always knock one off to *Home and Away* on a Friday night. I'd never hit Lillie's with a bullet in the chamber.'

Bulling: *adj.* demonstrating anger.

C

CABs: *noun, pl., abbr.* male, middle-aged bores who hang around golf or rugby club bars: Clubhouse Alpha Bores.

Can: *noun* the toilet.

C as M: *adj., abbr.* of low social status or demonstrating signs of this: common as muck. Example: 'Look at that! That woman's buying one of those wretched Lottery scratch cords!' 'C as M, Fionnuala! C as M!'

Cat: *adj.* (of a woman) ugly.

Celia Holman Lee: *noun, rhym.* attractive women, talent: gee [Celia Holman Lee is the head of a famous Limerick-based modelling agency.]

Chandler: *noun* someone, especially a man, who has difficulty committing himself to serious relationships. [Chandler Bing is a character in the US sitcom *Friends* (1994–2004).] Example: 'Have you heard from him?' 'No, not since Tuesday night.' 'Not even a text?' 'Nothing. I'm telling you, he is doing SUCH a Chandler on me.' 'Mind you, it's only Wednesday morning.' 'I suppose.' 'Hey, let's watch *Friends* on DVD and eat cake.'

Chariots of Fire: *noun* a game, particularly popular in rugby clubs, in which a length of toilet paper, usually five sheets, is inserted between the buttocks of each player, then lit. The last player to extinguish the fire is deemed the winner.

Chicken oriental: *adj., rhym.* mental.

Chillax: *verb* to become less tense or anxious; from conflation of 'chill' and 'relax'.

Chipper scum: *noun* socially disadvantaged people who exist on takeaway food, especially food that has been deep-fried in batter.

Chris Rea's Welsh cousin: *noun* a condition in which faeces is discharged from the bowels in liquid form: Dai Rea (diarrhoea). Example: 'Didn't see you at the Leinster match last night.' 'Yeah, I'd a touch of that Chris Rea's Welsh cousin. I was on the bowl all night.'

'That sounds like better entertainment than the match.'

Christian Andersens: *noun, pl.* hands, from Hans Christian Andersen. [Hans Christian Andersen (1805–75) was a children's author from Denmark who wrote such classics as 'The Ugly Duckling' and 'The Emperor's New Clothes'.] Example: 'Oh my God, I've just totalled the old man's Beamer. I'm not even allowed to, like, drive it and shit?' 'Looks like you've a major problem on your Christian Andersens, Dude.'

Chubby Chaser: *noun* a man with a penchant for women who are overweight.

CHV: *noun, abbr.* objectionable or contemptible people who live in local authority housing schemes: Council House Vermin.

Clip, nothing in the: (of a man) having no sexual desire. Example: 'I'd actually knocked one off ten minutes before the wife came home unexpectedly and suggested we go to bed. Well, Vicar, as you can well imagine, it was like walking into a gunfight with nothing in the clip.'
See also: Wankrupt.

Cliterati: *noun, pl.* a fashionable set of women.

Clobber: *noun* clothing, especially men's.

Columbo, a raincoat for: *noun* a condom. [*Columbo* was a popular 1970s US detective show starring Peter Falk.] Example: 'Oh, I want you! I want you! Yes! Yes! Take me! Take me now!' 'Hey, hold your horses. I'm just going to grab a raincoat for Columbo.'
See also: Johnny B. Goods; Love zeppelin.

Communists: fallen to the Communists: the condition of menstruating. Example: 'I've just seen your bird, Dude. She does NOT look a happy camper.' 'What do you expect? She's fallen to the Communists.' 'Nightmare.' 'Once a month, Dude. Once a month.'
See also: Blocks, up on the; Munster are playing at home; Painters; Period costume drama.

Conkers deep: *adj.* having achieved full penetration during sexual intercourse.

Conniption: *noun* a fit of rage or hysterics. Example: 'Oh my God, Sophie is having a TOTAL conniption because you scored that goy she likes.' 'I actually don't care. He was great. He's hung like a hoover, by the way.' 'So I heard. Oh my God.'

Contented temporary tent-dweller: *noun* someone experiencing happiness or pleasure; not a contented temporary tent-dweller, someone who is annoyed about something.
See also Happy camper.

Cop: *verb* notice.

Cor: *noun* car.

Corporate box: *noun* well-dressed, professional women.

Crash and burn: *verb* to fail publicly and spectacularly in an effort to chat up someone.

Cream: *verb* 1. to knock someone down forcibly; 2. to cream oneself: to become excited to the point of ejaculation.

Cream cracker: *noun, rhym.* a person of low social status: Knacker. Creamer, *abbr.*

Cripple juice: *noun* strong liquor.
See also: Idiot juice.

Crouching Tiger: *noun, abbr.* a small bottle of vodka smuggled into a pub or underage nightclub and then used to top up soft drinks from the alcohol-free bar: Crouching Tiger, Hidden Naggin.

Crufts: *noun* a derogatory term for a nightclub or school with a higher proportion of ugly females than pretty ones.

Cut someone's lunch: *verb* to steal the attentions of a girl who was in the process of being chatted up by another male.

D4 head: *noun* a silly or foolish girl: Dumb, Ditsy and Dependent on Daddy.

Daggers: *noun* venomous looks, especially from a woman: give daggers; *verb* to deliver such a look. *See also:* Filthy.

Damien, up the: *adj.* having a child developing in the uterus [Brit. Aus. *informal*, Up the duff]: Damien Duff. [Damien Duff is a soccer player who plays for Ireland.] *See also*: Ballyjames.

Dance card: *noun* a person's sexual history. Example: 'Hey, Dude, I have all of the O'Prey sisters on my dance card.'

Daniel Day: *noun, rhym.* the Luas, a suburban light-rail system that serves Dublin: Daniel Day-Lewis. [Daniel Day-Lewis is an Irish-born actor who won an Oscar for his performance as Christy Brown in *My Left Foot*.] Example: 'Are you driving into town?' 'Nah, fock it, I think I'll get the old Daniel Day.' 'Cool, that way you can get mullered.' Danny Day, *abbr.*

Deck: *verb* to knock somebody to the floor with a punch: decked; *adj.* the state of having been knocked to the floor with a punch.

Deep Heat: *noun, pl., rhym.* feet.

Denis: *noun* a purple bruise caused by a lover kissing or sucking the skin: a hickey: Denis Hickie. [Denis Hickie is an Ireland rugby international.]

Diner's remorse: *noun* the feeling of deep regret that comes over a woman when a fellow diner's order looks more appetizing than her own.
See also: Food envy.

Ditchpig: *noun* an extremely ugly woman.
See also: Moonpig.

DNS: *noun, abbr.* North Dublin, particularly the socially disadvantaged part: d'north side /de nort soyid/.

Doggy lipstick: *noun* a dog's erection. Also in the abbreviated form, lipstick.

Donald: have a Donald *noun, rhym.* to defecate, to take a dump: Donald Trump.

Drain the lizard: *verb* (of a man) to urinate.

Drico: *noun* Brian O'Driscoll. [Brian O'Driscoll is the captain of the Ireland rugby team and the 2005 Lions.] Also the Dricster, Dricmeister, Dricmeister General.

Drop anchor in Porcelain Bay: *verb* to discharge faeces from the body into a toilet.
See also: Drop the kids off at the pool; Drop the shopping.

Drop biscuits: *verb* to emit gas from the anus.

Drop the kids off at the pool: *verb* to discharge faeces from the body in a very hurried manner.
See also: Drop the shopping; Drop anchor in Porcelain Bay.

Drop the shopping: *verb* to discharge faeces from the body in a very hurried manner.
See also: Drop anchor in Porcelain Bay; Drop the kids off at the pool.

Dubes: *noun, pl.* Dubarry Docksiders, a brand of hand-stitched, leather boat shoe popular in South Dublin.

Dublin: *adj.* a euphemism to describe someone of a low social status. Example: 'Our new cleaner, she's really nice, but she's REAL Dublin.'

Dublin 4: *noun* the most desirable postcode in Dublin.

Dublin (twenty) 4: *noun* the least desirable postcode in Dublin, Tallaght.

Dublin 4 (teen): *noun* Dundrum.

Dude: *noun* a man, a guy.

Dulchie: *noun* A native Dubliner who lives and commutes to the city from the new dormitory suburbs in counties Wicklow, Kildare or Meath.

E

Eartha: *have an Eartha verb, rhym.* to defecate, to shit: Eartha Kitt. [Eartha Kitt (b. 26 January 1928) is an American-born singer and actress whose coquettish, self-deprecating style recalls that of Marlene Dietrich.] Example: 'Dorling, I'm heading upstairs for an Eartha Kitt. I might be some time.' 'Okay, I'll pop a toilet roll in the fridge.' 'God, I love you.'

Easy like Sunday morning: *noun* the state of being relaxed and untroubled. [From the hit single 'Easy' by The Commodores (1977).]

Edge-of-the-bed virgin: *noun* a girl who seems keen to have sexual intercourse for the first time, but then at the last minute insists on engaging in a long period of soul-searching on the subject.

Eppo: *noun, abbr.* a fit of rage or anger, from epileptic fit.

Exes and Ohhhs: *noun* a game in which males try to bed as many of their former girlfriends as they can over a specified period of time.

Eye, wipe someone's: *verb* to beat another male in a contest to sleep with the same girl.

Feds: *noun, abbr.* the Gardaí, the Irish police, from Federal Bureau of Investigation (US).

Feed the toothless donkey: *verb* to unsuccesfully try to achieve sexual arousal in a woman using one's hand.

Filthy: *noun* a venomous look, especially from a woman: give a filthy or filthies; *verb* to deliver such a look.
See also: Daggers.

Five-knuckle shuffle: *noun* the act of masturbating.

Fleck: *noun* someone of low social standing.
See also: Ken Acker; Knacker; Skanger; Skobie.

Fleck Republic: *noun* a generic term used to describe a socially disadvantaged area.
See also: Knackeragua.

Flick: *verb* give the flick: to break-up with a boyfriend or girlfriend, usually in a cruel and cursory fashion.

Flicks: *noun* the cinema.

Flick the Vs: *verb* to make a V-shape from one's index and middle finger as a gesture of abuse or contempt.

Flipper: *noun* a female with a history of engaging in relationships with men who later discover they're gay.

Floor: *verb* to press down hard on the accelerator pedal of a car.

Flying waitress: *noun* an air-hostess.

Folding green: *noun* money.

Food envy: *noun* the jealous feeling that comes over a woman when a fellow diner's order looks more appetizing than her own.
See also: Diner's remorse.

Foxrock tractor: *noun* an SUV, a high-performance, four-wheel-drive vehicle.

Fresher: *noun* a first-year student in college, from fresh meat.

Funbags: *noun* a woman's breasts.
See also: Airbags; Lung capacity; Rack; Top tens; Walters.

Funbundle: *noun* an aesthetically pleasing girl, particularly one with large breasts.

G

Gaff: *noun* a house.

Gag: *verb* to want something desperately, usually sex: gagging for it.

GAL: *abbr.* an exclamation to convey that someone is being petty or ridiculous: Get A Life.

Geebag gumboots: *noun* knee-high boots worn by women, often of low moral virtue.
See also: Slut wellies.

George Hook: *noun, rhym.* 1. a lascivious look. [George Hook is an Irish rugby pundit and drivetime radio host.] Example: 'That bird there is giving me big-time George Hooks.' 'Hey, that's my sister.' 'Live with it, Dude.' *noun, rhym.* 2. a malicious look.

Gick, the: *noun* a nickname or term of abuse for Terenure College, a prestigious South Dublin secondary school famous for playing rugby. Terenure > Nure > Manure > Gick.

Girvinator, the: *noun* Girvan Dempsey, the Leinster and Ireland rugby full-back.

God botherers: *noun, pl.* strangers who try to talk to you about religion, especially the ones who call to your door.

Godot: *noun* a female who is unwilling or unable to become sexually aroused, a woman who never climaxes, no matter how long you wait. [*Waiting for Godot* is an absurdist play by the Irish Nobel Prize-winner Samuel Beckett, which was first published in 1952.]

Golden goal: *noun* an unexpected sexual encounter that originates after closing time at a bus stop, taxi rank or fast-food outlet.

Grandington: *noun* 1,000.

Grant Mitchell's phone: *adj.* out of order. Example: 'Sorry, Dude, I scored your ex last night.' 'You're Grant Mitchell's phone, my friend.' 'What can I say? She was all over me.'

Gregory Peck: *noun, rhym.* neck. [Gregory Peck (5 April 1916–12 June 2003) was an American film actor who won the Best Actor Oscar for his role in the 1961 classic *To Kill A Mockingbird*.]

H

Hairy cyclops: *noun* the male genital organ.

Hand Solo: *noun* the act of masturbating.

Hanging: *adj.* hungover. Example: 'I am seriously hanging here.' 'What was that shit we were drinking anyway?' 'Brake fluid.'

Hank: *adj., rhym.* hungry, starving: Hank Marvin. [Hank Marvin (b. Brian Robson Rankin, 28 October 1941) was a guitarist with the popular instrumental band The Shadows. They began life as the backing group for Cliff

Richard, but achieved success in their own right in the late 1950s and early 1960s, between the demise of skiffle and the emergence of R 'n' B and Merseybeat.]

Happy bo bappy: *adj.* feeling or showing pleasure or contentment.

Happy camper: *noun* someone experiencing pleasure or contentment; not a happy camper, someone who is annoyed about something.
See also: Contented temporary tent-dweller.

Harrelson: *noun* an erection, or 'woody': Woody Harrelson. [Woody Harrelson is an American actor who has starred in such films as *Natural Born Killers* and *The People vs Larry Flint*.] Example: 'I can't wait for you to meet my grandmother. Oh my God, here she comes. Stand up.' 'Shit! I can't! I've got a dirty big Harrelson on me.'

Head-wrecker: *noun* (of a person or relationship) demanding a lot of patience or attention.

Heddild: *noun* The *Evening Herald*, a popular newspaper among Dublin's lower social classes.

High-five: *noun* a gesture of celebration or greeting in which two people slap each other's open palms with their arms raised; *verb* to perform such a gesture.

Hillbilly Idiot Juice: *noun* bourbon.

Hit and miss: *noun, rhym.* a piss.

Homemade soup, a face like: *noun* (of a woman) ugly.

Honey: *noun* a sexually attractive woman.

Horndog: *noun* a man or woman with a particularly large sexual appetite.

Horrendufied: *adj.* drunk to the point of being unable to stand. Example: 'I can't make it into work today, boss. I was focking horrendufied last night. I'm still a bit pissed this morning actually.' 'That's okay . . . and don't call me boss – it's Dad.'
See also: Mullered; Transmogrified; Trousered.

Horse: *verb* to eat greedily, as if from a nosebag.

Hospital pass: *noun* a poor pass in rugby that places the receiver in mortal danger.

Hots, the: *noun* an attraction.

Hound: *noun* an ugly or unsightly woman.

Howiya: *noun* a person of low social standing, from the greeting popular in socially disadvantaged parts of Dublin.

Huggy Bear: *noun* cool, calm. [Huggy Bear was a character in the 1970s American TV show *Starsky and Hutch* who was renowned for his coolness.] Example:

'This is a big game. You must be kacking it.' 'No, I'm actually Huggy Bear at the moment.'

Hum: *noun* smell.

Hurl: *verb* to vomit; *noun* any matter vomited from the stomach.

I

Ice queen: *noun* a female with a frosty demeanour.

Idiot juice: *noun* strong liquor.
See also: Cripple juice.

Ivana Trump: *noun, rhym.* to defecate, a dump.

J

J1er: *noun* a summer trip to the United States made by Irish students for the purposes of finding work, named after the temporary work visa they require to do this.

Jackanory: *noun* story: What's the Jackanory? What's happening? [*Jackanory* was a popular children's television programme in the 1970s and 1980s, revived in 2006.]

Jack Palance: *noun, rhym.* a dance. [Jack Palance (18 February 1919–10 November 2006) was an

American actor who was nominated for the Best Supporting Actor Oscar for his roles in *Sudden Fear* and *Shane* in the early 1950s. He finally landed the coveted statuette forty years later, after playing two parts, those of identical twins **Curly and Duke**, in the movie *City Slickers*.]

Jack Rowell: *noun, rhym.* a towel. [Jack Rowell is a former coach of the England rugby team.]

Jacobs: *noun, pl., rhym.* testicles, knackers: Jacob's Cream Crackers.

Jammer: *noun, rhym.* car: Jam jar.

Jammers: *adj.* full of people, especially a pub.

Japanese helicopter pilot, play the: *verb* to masturbate furiously, especially with one's mouth open and one's eyes closed.

Javelin: *noun* the male genital organ; *verb* throw the javelin: to have sexual intercourse with someone.

J. Edgar: *noun* a vacuum cleaner: J. Edgar Hoover. [John Edgar Hoover (1895–1972) was the director of the FBI from 1924 until the time of his death. He is credited with organizing the bureau into an efficient law enforcement agency, but was criticized for the part he played in the McCarthy Communist witch-hunts.]

Jizz: *noun* the male reproductive fluid, containing spermatozoa in suspension.

Jizz rag: *noun* a piece of cloth, especially a sock, that's used to mop up after an act of masturbation.

John B.: *adj.* keen: John B. Keane. [John B. Keane was an Irish playwright.] Example: 'Look at the state of that bird.' 'I wouldn't be too John B. on her myself.' 'A focking sniper wouldn't take her out.'
See also: Terry.

Johnny B. Goods: *noun* condoms, rubber johnnies.
See also: Columbo, a raincoat for; Love zeppelin.

Johnny Cashes: *noun, pl.* girls who wear an excess of fake tan, giving their faces an orangey glow. [Johnny Cash (26 February 1932–12 September 2003) was a highly influential American country and rock 'n' roll singer and songwriter, whose hits included 'Orange Blossom Special'.]

Jump: *verb* to have sexual intercourse with.

K

K: *noun* (pl. Ks) 1,000. Example: 'How much was your cor?' 'Sixty Ks.' '*Sixty Ks?* You must be loaded.' 'No, but my old man is.' 'Same thing.'

Kack it: *verb* to experience extreme nervousness or anxiety.

Kacks: *noun* 1. trousers; 2. a man's underpants; 3. a woman's knickers.

K Club: *noun* 1. a golf and country club in Straffan, County Kildare; 2. Kielys, a pub in Donnybrook, County Dublin.

Keith: *noun* an erection: Keith Wood: woody. [Keith Wood is the former captain of the Ireland rugby team.] Example: 'I've had a dirty big Keith on me since the second that focking Gráinne Seoige walked in.' 'Dorling, this is supposed to be our anniversary dinner.' 'Oh, yeah.'

Ken: *noun, abbr.* Heineken, a brand of lager, popular in South Dublin, that originated in the Netherlands.

Ken Acker: *noun, abbr.* a personification of a socially disadvantaged Dubliner, represented as a man with a wispy moustache, a Celtic shirt and numerous tattoos and sovereign rings. Knacker > K'nacker > Ken Acker. *See also:* Fleck; Knacker; Skanger; Skobie.

Kick-ass: *verb* to achieve what one has set out to do with ease; *adj.* kick-ass: extremely good, outstanding. Example: 'It's not easy being a kick-ass rugby player, you know.'

Kiddy-nipper: *noun* 1. a young person; 2. an underage drinker.

Kipper: *noun* someone, especially a girl, with red hair.

Klingon: *noun* someone who attaches himself or herself to company and is oblivious to the fact that he or she is not wanted.

Knacker: *noun* someone of low social standing.
See also: Fleck; Ken Acker; Skanger; Skobie.

Knackeragua: *noun* a generic term to describe any disadvantaged part of Dublin.
See also: Fleck Republic.

Knackerydoo: *noun* a nickname for Club 92, a popular South Dublin nightclub.

Knicker-fit: *noun* a fit of anger or histrionics, especially by a woman. Example: 'You said you'd be home at ten o'clock!' 'Hey, don't have a knicker-fit, Babe.'

Knob: *verb* (of a man) to have sex with someone; *noun* a boring, studious or socially inept person.

Knob chopper: *noun* a toilet seat that won't stay in the upright position.

Kool-Aid, drink the: *verb* to remain calm and unperturbed. [Kool-Aid is a popular brand of carbonated soda manufactured and sold mostly in the US.]

Kool and the Gang: 1. exclamation used to express agreement or satisfaction; 2 *noun*. the state of being calm and at ease. Example: 'Have you got a problem with that?' 'Hey, Dude, I'm Kool and the Gang.'

L

Lagging jacket: *noun* a condom.

Lambay rules: a code of honour among males that says whatever embarrassing incidents occur during the course of a holiday aren't mentioned again on their return: what happens beyond Lambay Island stays beyond Lambay Island [traditionally a code among Irish sailors].

Lead-foot: *verb* to drive with one's foot hard on the accelerator; *noun* someone who drives in this way.

Ledge: *noun, abbr.* a person worthy of the most lavish praise; a legend.

Length, throw a: *verb* (of a man) to have sexual intercourse with a woman.

Leons: *noun* diarrhoea: Leon Trotsky, the trots. [Leon Trotsky (7 November 1879–21 August 1940) was a Bolshevik revolutionary and Marxist theorist who was influential in the formation of the Soviet Union but was murdered in Mexico City after falling out with Joseph Stalin.]

Liberate: *verb* to borrow or steal. Example: 'Hey, Dude, I liberated the old man's credit cord from his wallet.' 'Cool. Let's go lapdancing.'

Lick the pot: *verb* to succeed in relation to chatting up or bedding many women. Example: 'How did you get on at Sally Prunty's twenty-first?' 'Hey, I licked the pot.' 'Wow. You rock.' 'I know.'

Lid: *noun, rhym.* a euro: quid. Example: 'Dad, I need three hundred lids.' 'What happened to the five hundred I gave you last Saturday?' 'Forget it, then, you scab.'

Lionel: *noun, rhym.* hair: Lionel Blair. [Lionel Blair was a dancer and popular television presenter in the 1970s and 1980s.]

Lips, throw the: *verb* to kiss. Example: 'I threw the lips on that bird from Glenageary last night.' 'No focking way! She's, like, SO hot, man.' 'I know.'

Little boy locked, play: *verb* to pretend to be drunker than one is to bring out the mothering instinct in a wife or girlfriend and thus avoid a bollocking.

Liza Minnelli: *noun, rhym.* the telly. [Liza Minnelli (b. 12 March 1946) is an American singer and actress who

in 1972 won the Best Actress Oscar for her role in
Cabaret. She is the daughter of Judy Garland.]
See also: Savalas.

Loaded gun: *noun* the condition of the male genital
organ when ejaculation hasn't occurred in some time.
Example: 'I'm going to whack off before I go out.' 'Are
you crazy? What if you score later?' 'Never go out with
a loaded gun, my friend. That's how mistakes are
made.'

Loads, give it: *verb* 1. to cheer in a boisterous manner;
2. to turn on the charm in one's efforts to chat up a
girl.

LOL: *text, abbr.* an exclamation meaning, 'I'm laughing
out loud.'

Loosener: *noun* a drink, or often more, to kick-start a
night out.

Loser: *noun* a person who is socially unsuccessful.

Love zeppelin: *noun* a condom.
See also: Columbo, a raincoat for; Johnny B. Goods.

Lubricated: *adj.* drunk.

Lung capacity: *noun* a woman's breasts, especially
large ones.
See also: Airbags; Funbags; Rack; Top tens; Walters.

M

Mac attack: *noun* a make-over, especially from the Mac counter in a department store.

Malcolm: *noun, rhym.* belly: Malcolm O'Kelly. [Malcolm O'Kelly is a second-row forward on the Ireland international rugby team.] Example: 'We shouldn't have had those falafels last night. The old Malcolm's giving me fierce gyp this morning.'

Mall Teaser: *noun* a girl who spends time hanging out in shopping centres, flirting with boys.

Mare: *noun, abbr.* a bad time: a nightmare. Example: 'St Michael's had a total mare against Pres Bray, of all schools.' 'Bray! Slot-machine City! How humiliating!'

Margaret: *noun, rhym.* bed, scratcher: Margaret Thatcher.

Marilyn, the: *noun* The Ballymun Road in North Dublin. Known locally as the Mun Road or, to South Dubliners making the daily trip to Dublin City University, the Marilyn Mun Road.

Matinée: *noun* sexual intercourse in the middle of the day, especially the afternoon; *verb* give the matinée: to have sexual intercourse with someone in the middle of the day. Example: 'Dude, your face is majorly red.' 'Yeah, I was just giving Jennie with an ie a matinée.'

'But she's got a face like a bucket of smashed crabs.'
'I know. I'm not proud of myself.'

Maxed out: *adj.* (of a credit card) having reached or exceeded its credit limit.

MDB: *verb, abbr.* Managing Daddy's Business. Example: 'Nice cor – did you rob a bank or something?' 'No, I'm doing an MDB, my friend.' 'Nice work – if your dad can get you it.'

Menstrually disturbed: *adj.* having little or no ability to reason due to the imminence or onset of menstruation.

Menstrually handicapped: *adj.* the condition of being unwilling or unable to engage in sexual intercourse due to the imminence or onset of menstruation.

Mickey Marbh: *noun* Stillorgan, a South Dublin suburb. Gaelic: Dead Mickey.

Mickey Tuesday: *noun* the day of the month when single mothers' allowance is paid out, traditionally the easiest night in Dublin to get casual sex.

MILF: *noun, abbr.* the attractive mother of a friend: Mother I'd Like to Fock.

Mince Pies: *noun, rhym.* eyes; *verb* give mince pies: to cast someone amorous looks.

Minger: *noun* a female who is ugly or hard on the eye.

Moby: *adj., rhym.* sick: Moby Dick.

Moolah: *noun* money.

Moonpig: *noun* an extremely ugly woman.
See also: Ditchpig.

Moonwalk: *verb* to walk backwards, in a smooth, gliding manner, often out of a girl's bedroom.

Morkeshing: *noun* marketing.

Morto: *adj., abbr.* embarrassed; mortified.

Mosey: *verb* walk or move in a leisurely manner.

Mulchie: *noun* a native of the Irish countryside.

Mullered: *adj.* very drunk.
See also: Horrendufied; Transmogrified; Trousered.

Munster are playing at home: (of a woman) the act or condition of menstruating. [Munster are an Irish rugby team whose home colour is red.] Example: 'I'm sorry I threw that television at you, Dorling. You know what I'm like when Munster are playing at home.'
See also: Blocks, up on the; Communists; Painters; Period costume drama.

Mutt: *noun* an ugly girl bearing a strong resemblance to a dog. Example: 'I know what I said last night. That was before I realized you were a mutt.'

My First Lager: *noun* the half-pint pots of beer they drink in Australia. Also known as Fisher-Price beers.

N

Nads: *noun, pl., abbr.* testicles: gonads.

Natalie: *noun* a working-class female.

Nat King: *noun, rhym.* sex; *verb* to get one's Nat King: to engage in sexual intercourse with someone: Nat King Cole. [Nat 'King' Cole (b. Nathaniel Adams Coles, 17 March 1919–15 February 1965) was a jazz singer who enjoyed pop-chart success with hits such as 'Mona Lisa' and 'When I Fall In Love'.]

Neck: *verb* to drink, especially alcohol, straight from the bottle.

Nip: *verb* to kiss.

Northside Shower: *noun* a can of Lynx deodorant.

Nosebag: *noun* food.

No stranger to a fish supper: *adj.* (of a person) fat.

NQR: *abbr.* Not quite right. Example: 'There's something NQR about that bird Conor's scoring at the moment.' 'Is it the moustache?' 'Yeah, that's it – you've put your finger on it.'

O

Oil tanker: *noun, rhym.* an objectionable person: wanker.

OMG: *text, abbr.* an expression meaning, 'Oh my God!'

One-eared Space Hopper, play with the: *verb* to masturbate.

One-eyed love warrior: *noun* the male genital organ.

One-eyed zipper fish: *noun* the male genital organ.

One F: *noun* Derek Foley, rugby correspondent for *The Star* newspaper in Ireland.

One in the post: *noun* a fart that refuses to be held back. Example: 'Sorry, Babes, I know it's our wedding and shit, but I'm going to have to, like, step outside. I've got one in the post.'

ONO: *abbr.* a one-night stand: One Night Only.

Orse: *noun* a person's buttocks or anus: arse (Brit.).

Orts: *noun* subjects of study primarily concerned with the processes and products of human creativity and social life, such as languages, literature and history.

Ossified: *adj.* the condition of being very drunk.

P

Pad: *noun* a house or apartment.

Padraig: /*Paw-rig*/*adj., rhym.* (of a smell) fierce, pungent, overpowering: Padraig Pearse [Padraig Pearse (1879–1916) was the commandant general of the Irish Volunteers, who staged the 1916 rebellion known as the Easter Rising. He proclaimed the Republic from the GPO and signed the order to surrender five days later. He was executed.] Example: 'Oh My God, the smell in here is Padraig.'

Painters: to have the painters in: *adj.* the condition of menstruating. Example: 'Oh My God, I've some focking appetite for Mars Bars today. And stabbing men. It's probably because I've the painters in.'
See also: Blocks, up on the; Communists; Munster are playing at home; Period costume drama.

Pant Python: *noun* the male genital organ.

Pauline: *noun, abbr.* a foul mood: Pauline Fowler. [Pauline Fowler was a character in the popular British television soap *EastEnders*, known for her lack of bonhomie.] Example: 'What are you doing in the battle cruiser on a Tuesday night?' 'Ah, I had to get away from herself. She's in a right Pauline.'

PCS: *noun* a condition that causes girls to dig their nails into a boyfriend or husband when they're not receiving what they consider sufficient attention: Purring Cat Syndrome.

Peg: *verb* to run or move at a fast rate: peg it.

Pen: *noun, rhym*. stink: pen and ink.

Period costume drama, to have a starring role in a: *verb* to menstruate. Example: 'Not playing tennis this morning, Sophie?' 'Not today, I'm afraid. I've got a starring role in a period costume drama.' 'It's funny, on all those tampon ads, the girls seem to stay pretty active during their periods.' 'Get out of my focking way or I'll stab you.'
See also: Blocks, up on the; Communists; Munster are playing at home; Painters.

Perry: *noun* a coma: Perry Como [Perry Como (b. Pierino Como, 18 March 1912–12 May 2001) was a crooner, heavily influenced by Bing Crosby, who sold 20 million records and whose most famous hits were 'Don't Let The Stars Get In Your Eyes' (1953), 'Catch A Falling Star' (1958) and 'Hot Diggity (Dog Ziggity Boom)' (1956).]

Peter: *noun, rhym.* a tan, caused by exposure of the skin to the sun: Peter Pan.

Petty Pilfering: *noun* a social game, popular among boys and young men, the object of which is to steal CDs that are particularly lacking in taste or style from the bedrooms of as many female conquests as possible.

Phileas Fogg: *noun* a taxi journey in which the driver takes an unnecessarily long and circuitous route in order to run up a higher fare on the meter. Also known as Around the World in Eighty Minutes. [Phileas Fogg is a character in the book *Around the World in Eighty Days* (1873), by Jules Verne.]

Pick a lock: *verb* the act of seducing a woman. Example: ' A good nosebag in Shanahan's is the key that picks her lock.'

Picture, no sound: *adj.* (of a person) attractive, but with nothing to say.

Pissing into the wind: *verb* wasting one's time, especially when chatting up a woman.

Plastic surgeon: *noun, rhym.* a virgin.

Play off the big centre-forward: *verb* to become sexually involved with a female who is already in a relationship. Example: 'How's it working out with that Carol, Dude? You still playing off the big centre-forward?' 'Yeah. I mean, her boyfriend takes all the knocks, the elbows and the rough treatment – and I do the scoring.'

PONPA: *abbr.* a relationship conducted in a surreptitious manner: Private Only, No Public Appearances.

Pop: *noun* alcohol, especially beer. Example: 'My problem is I like my pop too much.' 'No, your problem is I've just caught you in bed with my wife and I'm going to tear you a new orsehole.'

Pork javelin: *noun* the male genital organ; *verb* throw the pork javelin: to have sexual intercourse with someone.

Pot roast: *noun* love handles, deposits of excess fat on a person's waistline.

Pram springs: *noun* a generic term to describe any socially disadvantaged part of Dublin with a high number of single teenage mothers.

Prob: *noun, abbr.* Carlsberg, a popular lager brewed in Denmark, from the advertising slogan, 'Probably the best lager in the world'.

Putty in the hand: *noun* of persuadeable virtue.

R

Rack: *noun* a woman's breasts.
See also: Airbags; Funbags; Lung capacity; Top tens;
Walters.

Ran-a-lites: *noun, pl.* Dublin 6 rich-kid boy-racers,
especially from Ranleagh.

Randolph Scotts: *noun, pl., rhym.* spots: Randolph
Scott. [Randolph Scott (23 January 1898–2 March
1987) was an American film actor who starred in such
movies as *Gung Ho!*, *Western Union* and *Rebecca of
Sunnybrook Farm*.]

Randomer: *noun* (derogatory) someone who is
unknown to people in a particular social group.
Example: 'Who was that goy Katie was scoring in
Reynords last night?' 'I don't know – some total
randomer.'

Rattle: *verb* to have sex with someone; *noun* the act
itself. Example: 'I gave herself a seriously good rattle last
night. Woke up this morning and she cooked me a fry.'
'I like a woman who shows her gratitude.' 'So do I.'

Rattler: *noun* train.

Red cord: *verb* to end a relationship with someone,
often in a cruel manner, from the football expression, to
red card, or eject, a player from the field of play for a

serious breach of the rules. Example: 'Did you hear I red-corded Aoife last night? She was bawling her eyes out.' 'High-five, man!' 'Yes!'

Rents: *noun, pl., abbr.* parents.

Retord: *noun* 1. a mentally handicapped or retarded person, 2. a term of abuse used especially by teenage boys.

Reynords: *noun* Renards, an exclusive South Dublin nightclub.

Rhythms: *noun, pl., rhym.* shoes: rhythm and blues.

Rich tea: *adj.* (of a girl) plain.

Ricky Gervais: *noun, rhym.* face. [Ricky Gervais is a well-known comedy writer responsible for popular TV shows such as the Golden Globe-winning *The Office* and *Extras*.]

Ring, puke one's: *verb* to vomit violently.

Rip the piss: *verb* to joke, tease or hold someone or something up to public ridicule.

Rock and roll: *verb* get one's rock and roll: to have sexual intercourse.

Rod: *noun* an erection. Example: 'I've a rod on me that could empty lough Corrib.'

Rolling in it: *adj.* having a great deal of money.

Ronnie: *noun, abbr.* a moustache. Ronald Coleman. [Ronald Coleman (9 February 1891–19 May 1958) was a moustachioed English movie actor from the 1930s, 1940s and 1950s who won the Best Actor Oscar in 1947 for *A Double Life*.]

Roy Keane's dog: *noun* a compliant woman who's prepared to do anything to please her man; easy. [Roy Keane is a former Irish soccer player who famously walked a very obedient golden Labrador on television while his team-mates played in the World Cup.] Example: 'You don't seem to be putting in much spadework with Emily tonight?' 'Ah, she's Roy Keane's dog, Dude. She'll be trotting along home with me in half an hour, I'm telling you.'

Russell Harty: *noun, rhym.* party. [Russell Harty (5 September 1934– 8 June 1988) was a popular English television presenter in the 1970s and 1980s.]

S

S, the: *noun, abbr.* the senior rugby team in any school taking part in the Leinster, Munster, Ulster or Connacht senior cups.

Sack: *noun* bed.

Safe sex: *noun* sexual activity in which either partner takes the precaution of not giving the other their real phone number afterwards.

Sap: *noun* 1. a gullible person; 2. a socially awkward person.

Sauce: *noun* alcohol. Example: 'I probably should lay off the sauce. We've got a big match tomorrow.' 'Yeah – and we're only fourteen.'

Saucepan: *noun, rhym.* a kid: saucepan lid.

Savalas: *noun* telly, television: Telly Savalas. [Telly Savalas was an actor most famous for his role as Kojak in the US television cop show.]
See also: Liza Minnelli.

Scenario: *noun* attractive women.

Scooby Dubious: *adj.* dubious: Scooby-Doo. [*Scooby-Doo* was a popular US television cartoon from the 1970s and 1980s.] Example: 'If I keep playing the way I'm playing, there's no way Eddie O'Sullivan can leave me out of the Ireland squad.' 'I'd be a bit Scooby Dubious about that. I mean, you're, like, playing for Greystones' fifths.' 'Oh, yeah.'

Scoops: *noun, pl.* drinks, usually pints of lager.

SDP: *noun, abbr.* South Dublin Princess; a spoiled and stuck-up young woman from South of the Liffey.

Sean Connery: *noun, rhym.* a heart attack, a coronary.

September 10: *adj.* petty, pointless or irrelevant. Example: 'Claire is STILL going on about you scoring her boyfriend.' 'Oh my God, that is, like, SO September 10.' 'I know, it's like, GET over it, girl?'

Septic: *adj., rhym.* of or from the United States of America: Septic tank, Yank; *noun* a citizen of the United States of America.

Shabby: *adj.* hungover.

Sheets: *noun* euro.
See also: Shekels; Snots; Sponds; Squids; Yoyos.

Shekels: *noun* euro.
See also: Sheets; Snots; Sponds; Squids; Yoyos.

Sherman: 1. *noun, rhym.* bank; 2. *noun, rhym.* wank: Sherman tank.

S, H, I, T: *noun* shit.

Shit: *verb* to bullshit. Example: 'Do not shit me, Dude – was that really a goy I got off with last night?'

Shitfaced: *noun* drunk.

Shmugly: *adj.* ugly.

Shoecotic: *noun* a severe mental state in which women lose contact with external reality while thinking about shoes.

Shoot the shit: *verb* to chat.

Shopper's remorse: *noun* a feeling of deep regret or guilt, mostly felt by women, brought on by spending too much money.

Shot at the title: *noun* a chance or an attempt to have sexual intercourse with someone. Example: 'You see that bird over there – I'm thinking of giving her a shot at the title.' 'Which one? The one with the long curly black teeth?' 'Yeah.'
See also: Apollo Creed.

Shrapnel: *noun* loose change, usually that which is left after a night spent drinking in a pub or club.

Simon: *adj.* of the highest standard: Simon Best. [Simon Best is an Irish rugby international.]

Skanger: *noun* someone of low social standing.
See also: Fleck; Ken Acker; Knacker; Skobie.

Skobie: *noun* someone of low social standing.
See also: Fleck; Ken Acker; Knacker; Skanger.

Skobie tunic: *noun* a Celtic shirt.

Skobie Wan Kenobi: *noun* a nickname for a skobie.

Skull: *verb* to drink very quickly.

Slut wellies: *noun* knee-high boots worn by women, often of low moral virtue.
See also: Geebag gumboots.

Spit chunks: *verb* to vomit.

Snake-charming act: *noun* an erection. Example: 'So how did you get on with Melanie last night?' 'You won't believe this, but her old dear walked in while we were getting down to business. And she was not amused by my snake-charming act.'

Snoopster: *noun* Snoop Dogg, a popular rapper.

Snots: *noun* euro. Example: 'How much did your jacket cost you?' 'Eighty snots.' 'You could have got a new one for that.' 'Very focking funny.'
See also: Sheets; Shekels; Sponds; Squids; Yoyos.

So say: *noun, rhym.* bus: so say all of us.

Sovvy *noun* sovereign ring, worn by people of low social standing.

SP: *noun, abbr.* the situation: starting price.

Spadework: *noun* hard work, usually in chatting up a woman. Example: 'I put an hour of spadework into that bird Hannah and she ended up going off with the captain of Clongowes.' 'In fairness, though, you're ugly.'

Spanish Archer: *verb* give someone the Spanish Archer: to cast a lover aside in a cruel, cursory manner: El Bow.

Spew: *verb* to vomit.

Spin: *noun* a drive.

Splash: *verb* splash one's Dubes: to vomit.

Sponds: *noun* euro.
See also: Sheets; Shekels; Snots; Squids; Yoyos.

Squeeze the lizard: *verb* to discharge urine.

Squids: *noun* euro.
See also: Sheets; Shekels; Snots; Sponds; Yoyos.

Steamer: *noun* a homosexual.

Steaming: *adj.* feeling or demonstrating anger or annoyance.

Steeped: *adj.* lucky.

Steve Silvermint: *noun* the personification of coolness; *verb* play it like Steve Silvermint: to perform a task in a cool manner. [Steve Silvermint was a character in a 1980s TV advertisement for Silvermint sweets.]

Stoke: *noun, rhym.* homosexual, bent: Stoke-on-Trent.

Stormer: *noun* a good game, especially in rugby.

Straight red: get a straight red *noun* to be dumped by a boyfriend or girlfriend without warning.

Strop: *noun* a bad mood; *verb* have a strop on: to be in a bad mood. Example: 'Are you going into maths today?' 'Nah, I bumped into Ms White earlier. She's got a serious strop on.' 'Let's bunk off early and hit Stillorgan Shopping Centre.' 'Cool.'

Stud muffin: *noun* a young man regarded as a good or prolific sexual partner.

Suck the lips off: *verb* to kiss someone in an enthusiastic or vigorous manner.

Swamp donkey: *noun* an ugly girl.

Swiss: *noun, rhym.* sex, hole: Swiss roll. Example: 'I heard you've never had your Swiss.' 'Fock off!' 'Ever? In your whole life, like?' 'Sorry, do I know you?'

Sydney Parade: *noun* 1. a well-to-do suburb of South Dublin; 2. the last station before Sandymount when travelling northward on the Dart train. *Verb* get off at Sydney Parade: to use the withdrawal before ejaculation method of contraception.

T

Tallafornia: *noun* an ironic nickname for Tallaght, a populous and largely socially disadvantaged suburb of Dublin.

Tallafornication: *noun* sexual intercourse with someone from Tallaght.

Tanked: *adj.* drunk.

Taylor Keith: *noun, rhym.* teeth. [Taylor Keith is a brand of carbonated drinks popular in Ireland.]

Tear the back off: *verb* to speak ill of someone who isn't present.

Ten-four: exclamation used to express agreement or satisfaction.

Tennis racquet: *noun, rhym.* jacket.

Terry: *adj.* keen: Terry Keane. [Terry Keane was a notorious gossip columnist for the *Sunday Independent* in the 1980s and 1990s.]
See also: John B.

Textual intercourse: *noun* communication by SMS of a sexually suggestive or sexually explicit nature.

Theobald: *noun, rhym.* a phone: Theobald Wolfe Tone. [Theobald Wolfe Tone was the Protestant founder of the United Irishmen, who is regarded as the founding

father of Irish republicanism. In 1796 he tried to enlist French support for an abortive rising attempt. He was tried for treason and cut his own throat when his request to be shot like a soldier was refused.]
See also: Wolfe.

Thornley, Gerry: the rugby correspondent for *The Irish Times.*

Throw a bone: *verb* (of a man) to engage in sexual intercourse.

Throw the lips on: *verb* to kiss

TK Maxx: *noun, rhym.* toilet: jacks.

TK Nacks: *noun* nickname for TK Maxx, a department store that sells designer clothes at prices the lower social classes can afford.

TMI: *abbr.* an exclamation of revulsion or profound disgust when someone has related a story containing unnecessarily and usually nauseating details: Too Much Information. Example: 'Oh my God, I haven't eaten for so long, my gums are storting to bleed.' 'TMI, Chloë! TMI!'

Toast: *adj.* 1. dead; 2. in trouble. Example: 'Oh my God, I failed maths – I am focking toast.'

Tobler, on one's: *adv., abbr.* alone, on one's own: Toblerone. [Toberlone is a brand of popular confectionery containing chocolate, honey and almonds.] Example: 'I heard Sophie's going to the debs on her Tobler.' 'Yeah, that's since I dumped her orse.' 'Way to go, Dude.'

Tonsil hockey, play: *verb* to engage in a kiss in which one or both tongues deeply penetrate the other's mouth.

Tony Blair: *noun, rhym.* hair. [Tony Blair was the Prime Minister of Great Britain between 1997 and 2007.]

Tony Smeeth: *noun, rhym.* teeth.

Tool: *noun* 1. a penis; 2. a foolish or disagreeable person.

Top tens: *noun, rhym. pl.* a woman's breasts: top ten hits.
See also: Airbags; Funbags; Lung capacity; Rack; Walters.

Total: *verb* 1. to beat up; 2. to crash and write off a car.

Tosser: *noun* a stupid or irritating person.

Tosspot: *noun* a stupid or irritating person.

Town halls: *noun, rhym. pl.* testicles: balls.

Transmogrified: *adj.* very drunk.
See also: Horrendufied; Mullered; Trousered.

Trap: *noun* a cubicle in a public toilet. Example: 'Dude, where are you?' 'I'm in Trap Two.' 'Oh . . . fock, has something crawled up your orse and died!'

Trouser: *verb* to put something, especially money, into the pocket of your trousers.

Trousered: *adj.* drunk.
See also: Horrendufied; Mullered; Transmogrified.

Trouser gas: *noun* a fart. Example: 'Dude, did you let off trouser gas in here?' 'Yeah. I think I actually need medical attention.'

Trouser melons: *noun, pl.* deposits of excess fat at the sides of a person's waistline.

Trout: *noun* a woman, especially middle aged, who is unpleasing to the eye.

Truncheon: *noun* an erection. Example: 'I don't believe it, driver. This is my stop and I've a truncheon on me that could beat a donkey out of a quarry.' 'Looks like you're staying on all the way to the terminus, so.' 'That's just my luck! I hope it's not going to be another of those days again! I don't know!'

TUM: *noun, abbr.* an aesthetically unpleasing girl who will try to spoil the fun for her more attractive friends by

being hostile to any man who comes within their orbit: Token Ugly Mate.
See also: UBM.

Tumbleweed moment: *noun* a short instant in which everyone present is momentarily shocked into silence by the stupidity or inanity of something that has just been said or done.

U

UBM: *noun, abbr.* an aesthetically unpleasing girl who will try to spoil the fun for her more attractive friends by being hostile to any man who comes within their orbit: Ugly Best Mate.
See also: TUM.

Ugger Hugger: *noun* a man with a penchant for girls in UGG boots.

V

Vallys: *noun, abbr.* 1. Valentine's Day; 2. Valentine's Day cards.

VHI-positive: *adj.* (of a person) having or being covered by Voluntary Health Insurance.

Vom: *verb* to eject matter from the stomach through the mouth: to vomit; *noun* matter ejected in this way.

Von Trapp: *noun* mouth. Example: 'Have you finished your homework, Son?' 'Ah, shut your Von Trapp, you.'

W

Wagon: *noun* an overbearing or nagging woman.

Walk of shame: *noun* the long and lonely walk back to your friends after being red-carded by a girl you were trying to chat up.

Walters: *noun, rhym. pl.* woman's breasts: Walter Mitties, titties. [Walter Mitty was a fictional character famous for day-dreaming.]
See also: Airbags; Funbags; Lung capacity; Rack; Top tens.

Wankrupt: *adj.* (of a man) being unwilling or unable to perform sexually because of earlier masturbation.
See also: Clip, nothing in the.

Wardy: *noun* nickname for Tony Ward, Irish rugby international who now works as a rugby journalist with the *Irish Independent*.

Waters, overfish the: *verb* to deplete the stock of available women by spending too much time in one pub or nightclub.

Way: *adv.* very. Example: 'If you fell into a barrel of funbags, you'd come out sucking your thumb.' 'Dude, that's way harsh.'

WC: *adj., abbr.* (derogatory) working class.

Weapon of Mass Destruction: *noun* a particularly ugly female.

Wedge: *noun* money.

Wedgy: *noun* an act of mild torture, usually practised by schoolboys and adult rugby players, in which the victim's underpants are twisted until they snap, then removed from his body through the leg of his trousers; *verb* give a wedgy: to perform a wedgy on someone. *See also:* Atomic wedgy.

Weekend at Bernie's: *noun* someone who shows no signs of life at social occasions. [*Weekend at Bernie's* is a US movie (1989) in which two company executives take their murdered boss to a beach party and pass him off as alive.] Example: 'Did you see Amy's new boyfriend? He didn't talk to anyone all night.' 'I know. He's a total Weekend at Bernie's.'

Weight handicap: *noun* a girl who insists on accompanying her boyfriend on his nights out with his male friends.
See also: Yoko.

Wexican: *noun* a Dubliner who lives in Wexford.

Whatever: an exclamation used, usually by teenagers, to express frustration or scepticism.

Whip: *verb* to steal.

Wide-on: *noun* female arousal, the woman's equivalent of an erection. Example: 'That bird has a serious wide-on for me.' 'Why wouldn't she? She's human, isn't she?' 'Thanks, Dude.'

Wilsons: *noun, rhym. pl.* tickets: Wilson Picketts. [Wilson Pickett (b. 18 March 1941) is a soul singer who was popular in the 1960s and whose hits included 'In The Midnight Hour' (1965), 'Don't Fight It' (1965) and 'Mustang Sally' (1966).]

Winona: *noun* The Ryder Cup, a golf tournament played every two years between teams representing Europe and the United States. Example: 'Didn't see you at the Winona last weekend.' 'No, I was actually in bed with Winona Ryder.' [Winona Ryder is a Hollywood actress who has starred in such movies as *Heathers* and *Girl Interrupted*.]

Wolfe: *noun, rhym.* phone: Theobald Wolfe Tone. [Theobald Wolfe Tone was the Protestant founder of the United Irishmen, who is regarded as the founding father of Irish republicanism. In 1796 he tried to enlist French support for an abortive rising attempt. He was

tried for treason and cut his own throat when his request to be shot like a soldier was refused.]
See also: Theobald.

Wrecked: *adj.* 1. hungover; 2. ugly.

Wrist, one off the: *noun* the act of masturbation.

WTF: *text, abbr.* What the fock?

Wuss: *noun* a weak or ineffectual person.

Y

Yoko: *noun, abbr.* an overly possessive female who insists on accompanying her boyfriend everywhere, much to the displeasure or annoyance of his friends: Yoko Ono. [Yoko Ono was the then girlfriend – and later wife – of Beatles member John Lennon, who, during the recording of the album *Let It Be* (1969), virtually took up residence in the recording studio rather than leave his side, causing the inter-band tension that was considered one of the contributory factors in the eventual break-up of the band.] Example: 'I thought it was supposed to be just the goys going out tonight.' 'Sorry, Dude – she insisted on tagging along.' 'Oh my God, she is SUCH a Yoko. And she's bet-down.' 'Who

are you telling? You just have to drink with her. I'm engaged to the focking hag.'
See also: Weight handicap.

Yolk: *noun* an ugly female. Example: 'Oh my God, did you see the yolk I ended up with last night? I didn't know whether to ride her or milk her.'; *verb* to throw eggs at.

Yoyos: *noun* euro.
See also: Sheets; Shekels; Snots; Sponds; Squids.

Z

Zeppelin: *noun* a condom: love zeppelin.

Ross O'Carroll-Kelly's new book, *Mr S and the Secrets of Andorra's Box,* will be in bookshops all over South Dublin in October 2008. In fact, because Ross wants to do his bit for the underprivileged, it'll also be in bookshops beyond South Dublin. Here's a preview ...

The doorbell rings.

I throw on my Leinster training top and my boxer shorts, then tip down the stairs and open the door. It's obviously someone with the wrong address, roysh, because it's a bird – eighteen, maybe nineteen – and without wanting to come across as, like, racist here, she's black.

I go, 'Er, sorry, wrong gaff,' and I go to close the door in her face but just as I'm about to, roysh, she goes, 'I want to speak to Sorcha Lalor,' except the way she says it, it's like Soar-chah Lay-lor

I'm there, 'Soarchah Laylor's not here – what's all this about anyway?'

'Hello,' she goes, offering me her hand. 'My name is Immaculata Okonjo. I come from Nigeria. My home is a small village called Owu-Ijebu in the Ogun State, a hundred and forty-five miles east of Lagos. My mother and father died when I was a little girl, my mother from tuberculosis, my father from ischemic heart disease. I was six years old when I came to Owu-Ijebu. It is a small community with only twelve houses, a nursery, a primary school and a small clinic ...'

Lois and Clark is about to stort so I end up going, 'Is there much more of this?' and she looks at me sort of, like, confused. 'As in, can you get to the point?' I go.

'I am looking for Soarchah to thank her.'

'Thank her for what?'

'Because,' she goes, 'when I was six years old, she sponsored me.'

'Sponsored you? To do what?' She looks at me blankly. I'm there, 'A walk? A skipathon? You're a bit late coming around for the do-ray-me, aren't you?'

'No, no, no,' she goes. 'You don't understand. I mean she sponsored *me*. It was thanks to Soarchah that I was rescued from the streets of Lagos, where there are very bad men . . .'

Suddenly I'm like that focking Celine Dion, as in it's all coming back to me now. I actually remember her sponsoring a kid. She was a focking sucker for those ads on TV, especially if she liked the song – 'You Raise Me Up' or 'Flying Without Wings' or any of that focking muck.

There was always something about Westlife that made her want to set up direct debits.

Anyway, she sponsored her for years. I remember her trying to interest me in one or two of her letters – 'Oh my God, Ross, they've set up a small farming project, providing cassava and yams to storving children' – but obviously I'd fock-all interest.

'Sorcha's actually in the States,' I go. 'She's gone for pretty much a year . . .'

This look of, like, disappointment crosses her face, then for some reason I look down at her feet. She's got a suitcase with her.

It all of a sudden hits me that she has nowhere else to go.

'Why don't you come in,' I suddenly find myself going. And I don't know why because I don't *think* I want to score her.

I think I'm thinking, what would Sorcha do? She's been sponsoring her for ten years – I presume she'd take her in, at least until she got sorted with a hotel.

So I bring her in. I even carry her focking case for her. 'I'm Ross,' I go, doing the whole handshake thing.

She's like, 'Yes, I recognize you from the pictures Soarchah sent to me.'

I ask her if she fancies a cup of coffee. I was going to fire up the Nespresso. 'That would be nice,' she goes. 'You are very kind. Not like Soarchah described you to me ...'

Whoa, that rocks me back on my heels. I'm like, 'Really? What exactly did she say?'

'She said you slept with her sister and her friend before your wedding. She said you photocopied her notes for her special history topic at school and sold them on the internet. She said you gave her oral thrush for her eighteenth birthday ... 'Fock – up until that point I was going to ask her to produce her passport, just to prove she *was* who she *said* she was?

I'm like, 'I'm sure she must have told you one or two of the high points as well,' but she doesn't answer. She just storts mooching around the kitchen and dining room, looking at shit, going, 'You have a beautiful home. You are very lucky.'

'*Was* very lucky,' I go. 'Me and Sorcha, we're not actually together any more.'

'No!' she goes, genuinely horrified. She obviously hasn't written for a few months.

I'm there, 'Hey, it's cool. It was, like, mutual?' then I turn around and pop the capsule in the machine, a wedding present from Oisinn and one of the few good things to come out of our marriage.

She's like, 'So – Soarchah is gone to ...'

I'm there, 'The States. She's gone for a year. You probably should have written.'

She's standing in front of the contemporary bookshelf,

her head cocked to one side, reading the spines of all Sorcha's boxsets.

'What are these?' she goes.

I'm like, 'They're called, like, DVDs? They're pretty much like a CD except they've got, like, movies on them and shit?'

She gives me the duh-look then.

'I am from Nigeria,' she goes, 'not from outer space. What I mean is I have never heard of these movies. *Nip Tuck. Dawson's Creek. ER. The OC* . . .'

I'm there, 'The thing is they're not actual movies? They're, like, all her favourite TV programmes.'

'She watches all of these?'

I'm there, 'She does in her Swiss. If we ever experience, like, a nuclear winter, she might get around to it. Yeah, no, the thing with boxsets is you don't buy them to watch, you buy them to *own*?'

She suddenly gets, I don't know, frantic. 'I must watch them all,' she goes. 'I have so much to learn about Ireland.'

I'm like, 'Here, have one of these cookies. The ginger comes from some place in, I don't know, India. They pay the fockers a fortune for it as well . . .'

She takes one.

I go, 'Make yourself at home, Immaculata,' four words I didn't expect to be saying today. Sorry, five. 'You can stay here as long as you like.'

She gives me the most incredible smile then. 'You are a very nice man,' she goes.

I'm like, 'Separate beds, though.'

'Of course,' she goes, looking slightly confused. 'I have a boyfriend.'

I'm there, 'Believe me – I've been with a lot of birds who said that.'

381

ACKNOWLEDGEMENTS

Other contributions gratefully received from Teige MacCarthy-Morrow, Katie Ingle, Gillian Coffey, John O'Connor, Paddy Cahill, Paul Wallace, Alan Kelly, Ken Finlay, Tom Doorley and Dave McCann.

PHOTOGRAPH CREDITS

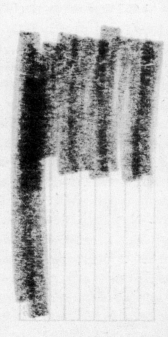

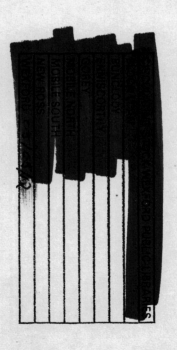